To my dear F̲ ̲ ̲ ̲ ̲
May God richly bless you
and keep you and may he
make his face to shine
upon you!

I AM WITH YOU ALWAYS

EXPERIENCING GOD IN TIMES OF NEED

CHIP INGRAM

Baker Books

A Division of Baker Book House Co
Grand Rapids, Michigan 49516

Published by Baker Books
a division of Baker Book House Company
P.O. Box 6287, Grand Rapids, MI 49516-6287

Published in association with Yates& Yates, LLP, Literary Agents, Orange, California

Printed in the United States of America

Library of Congress Cataloging-in-Publication Data

Ingram, Chip, 1954–
    I am with you always : experiencing God in times of need / Chip Ingram.
        p.   cm.
    Includes bibliographical references.
    ISBN 0-8010-1236-8
    1. Consolation. 2. Bible. O.T. Psalms—Devotional literature. I. Title.
    BV4905.3 .I54 2002
    242′ .4—dc21   2002003800

ISBN 0-8010-6452-X (intl. pbk.)

Published in association with Yates & Yates, LLP, Literary Agents, Orange, California.

For current information about all releases from Baker Book House, visit our web site:
http://www.bakerbooks.com

I dedicate this book to the body of believers at Santa Cruz Bible Church, who in the darkest nights of their soul have run to God and his Word and then had the courage to share both their pain and his grace.

CONTENTS

Acknowledgments   7
Introduction   8

1. When You Get a Raw Deal   11
    Psalm 73   18
    Experiencing God as Your Sovereign King   27
2. In Times of Crisis   43
    Psalm 23   52
    Experiencing God as Your Good Shepherd   68
3. When You Feel like a Nobody Going Nowhere   75
    Psalm 139   82
    Experiencing God as Your Loving Creator   101
4. When You Are Troubled and Depressed   107
    Psalm 77   121
    Experiencing God as the Lifter of Your Soul   135
5. When You Are Gripped by Fear   141
    Psalm 46   148
    Experiencing God as Your Refuge and Fortress   159
6. When You've Blown It Big Time   173
    Psalm 51   181
    Experiencing God as Your Forgiving Father   199

Contents

7. In Times of Confusion   205
    Psalm 90   214
    Experiencing God as Your Wise Counselor   236
8. God Is with You Always   239
    Experiencing God Always   249

    Notes   255

ACKNOWLEDGMENTS

First and foremost, I want to acknowledge the kindness and grace of a sovereign and good God who has allowed pain, suffering, and difficulty to enter my life at strategic points to draw me into deeper, richer, and more intimate relationship with himself and his Son, the Lord Jesus Christ.

I am also deeply indebted to my wife, Theresa, and our four children, Eric, Jason, Ryan, and Annie for their love, example, and encouragement during my times of need.

The project would have been impossible without the contributions of Connie Neal, Neil Wilson, and Vicki Crumpton who helped me take tapes, outlines, and manuscripts and turn them into clear, reliable chapters.

Closer to home, Annette Kypreos, my executive assistant, and Sealy Yates, my friend and literary agent, were both instrumental in taking a "great idea" and bringing it into reality.

My final acknowledgement is to those who pick this book up and read it in "their time of need" and meet God in a powerful way. My reward and joy is knowing I had the privilege of being a small part of that divine encounter.

INTRODUCTION

A moonless Texas night had settled on our neighborhood. It must have been a Saturday evening because I remember sitting on the living-room floor with my wife and kids while we folded the church bulletins for the Sunday service. Suddenly, ferocious barking erupted down the street and footsteps thudded up the walkway. Someone pounded on our door. I jumped up, ran to the door, and threw it open. There stood Michael, a friend of my older boys. He was sweaty and breathing hard. He looked like he'd just seen a ghost.

"Let me in! Let me in!" he pleaded, gasping for breath.

"What's wrong?" I asked.

"There's a huge dog. It's after me. It's going to kill me." Michael's body shook as he turned around to look for his assailant.

By now my whole family was at the door. The barking grew louder. We all stared, waiting for Michael's ferocious attacker. As I flipped on the porch light, a tiny dog bounded into view. His bark was bigger than his height! We all burst out laughing.

Now remember, it was pitch dark. Michael thought he was in grave danger because he couldn't see anything. The moment a little bit of light corrected his perception, he changed. He was relaxed and laughing with embarrassment.

At that moment I remember thinking how our perceptions always determine our actions. Michael thought he was in danger; he *felt a desperate need* to find a safe place. He knew he could take shelter at our house, so he dashed to our door.

We all have times like these. Most people run to God—almost instinctively. Even people who aren't too sure about God. Why? Somehow, we know deep down—or at least hope—that God will be our shelter.

I wrote this book to encourage you to run to God whenever

you get a raw deal and life just isn't fair,
you're going through a crisis or a major life transition,
you feel like a nobody going nowhere,
you're troubled and depressed,
you're gripped by fear,
you've blown it big time, or
you're confused.

God's Word, the Bible, will enable you to see your situation in a different way. It will flip on the porch light over your soul, so you can see what's really going on and what God would have you do about it. I'm telling you up front that God is *the* place to run. He is and has always been a shelter, a safe place where people can take refuge. God is real and ready to open his door to all who run to him in times of need.

Each chapter in this book looks at a specific need in light of one of the Psalms—the songbook of God's people. The Psalms are God-breathed, so they give truth and light. They were written by real people who didn't hold back their emotions. They dared to bring their desperate needs to God. Each chapter addresses a need common to us all. You may not have experienced all of them, but eventually you probably will. When these needs suddenly invade your life, I'd like you to know where you can turn in the Bible to find truth and encouragement. I also highlight an aspect of God's character that corresponds to the issue. And you will meet some special people along the way who have taught me by their lives, under extreme conditions, that they know God was with them.

I don't want you merely getting fresh ideas about God, nor do I want you simply to collect amazing secondhand stories about God's comforting presence. What I really want is for you to encounter the living God as he reveals himself to you. This is my prayer for you as we begin this journey together: "O Lord, open their eyes and let them see!"

I've borrowed this prayer from the ancient prophet Elisha. He used it on an occasion similar to the tough spot in which Michael found himself. The story is told in 2 Kings 6:8–23. Elisha and his servant were wanted men. The king of Aram had a contract out on their lives. Eventually, someone revealed their location to the king, and he sent an army by night to capture the prophet and his assistant. The soldiers quietly surrounded the village where Elisha was staying. When morning came, the servant left the house. Everywhere he looked there were armed men on horseback. Chariots, spears, and swords blocked every way of escape. Elisha and his companion were surrounded.

In shock and despair the servant called out to Elisha, "Ah, my lord, what will we do now?" (2 Kings 6:15b NLT). Instead of answering his servant's question, Elisha addressed his terror. "Don't be afraid. There are many more on our side than on theirs!" said the prophet. Before the servant could ask what he meant, Elisha lifted a prayer, "O Lord, open his eyes and let him see!"

"The Lord opened his servant's eyes, and when he looked up, he saw that the hillside around Elisha was filled with horses and chariots of fire" (2 Kings 6:17 NLT). The prophet's assistant caught a glimpse of ultimate reality. He learned a lesson that God allows each of us to learn throughout life: There is so much more to life than what we can see. Unless we can learn to expect God's continual presence in every part of life, we won't be able to experience his presence when we need it most. So again, my prayer for you as we begin is, "O Lord, open their eyes and let them see!"

I am with you . . .

WHEN YOU GET A RAW DEAL

S ome moments in our lives remain forever fresh. Like a scene from a movie embedded in our soul, we can recall with uncanny clarity every nuance of certain events that occurred years, even decades ago. The story I share here is one of those— an unforgettable, dramatic moment in my life when the world seemed very unfair. That moment left me so devastated, I was ready to forsake my relationship with God and quit the Christian life. But God met me in that time of need like never before.

I was twenty-one years old and had recently made the most difficult decision of my life. After months of struggle, I willfully chose to allow Christ to be the Lord of my life. It meant breaking off a relationship with a girl I loved deeply and had assumed would one day be my wife. We had dated for over two years and had done all the things you do when it's serious. I had visited her family on several occasions, and she had visited mine. We were both believers. We both loved God and loved each other more than anything or anyone we had ever known.

She was beautiful. We connected. We became great friends. She was all I ever dreamed a wife would be. But the more we talked about our life together, the clearer it became that an immovable object blocked our way. The dream in her heart pictured us living in a nice home with a white picket fence across the street from her mom and dad. She was an only child and was very close to her parents. She had a deep sense of responsibility toward them, and they were reaching their twilight years. I knew deep in my heart, even then, that God wanted to use my life in a way that would mean going wherever he called me, whenever he called. As much as I loved her, I knew marrying her was not God's will for me. The decision to break off our relationship in deference to the will of God was the greatest sacrifice I had ever been asked to make.

Even though I knew our breakup was right, it was excruciatingly painful. In my mind the choice was clear, but my emotions refused to catch up with the rest of me. After we broke up, I was a basket case for the better part of a year. I cried out for God to change her heart. I vividly recall sitting on a hill across from her dorm and begging God to let it work out for us to be together. I didn't date anyone else; I didn't want to. I secretly prayed and fasted, hoping that God was simply testing my loyalty. I trusted that just as God had given Abraham back his son Isaac, after he had been willing to sacrifice him, so God would give her back to me. Surely God would reward my faithfulness, I reasoned. Instead, God did the unthinkable.

The Raw Deal

It was late and I was tired. I played basketball on my college team, and a humiliating home game had just ended. I was emotionally down, physically fatigued, and spiritually frustrated as I trudged up two flights of stairs from the locker room to the exit. With my hair still wet and my jacket over my shoulder, I looked up to see a sight I hadn't seen in months. Standing at the top of the stairs was my former girlfriend. She was waiting in our spot, next to the railing where she always used to meet me after home games. I could hardly believe my eyes! Instantly I thought, "God has answered my prayers! She is standing there waiting for me, just like the good old days." As the adrenaline and joy surged through me, I started making plans. We'd go get a bite to eat, and she'd tell me how God had changed her mind about our future.

As the distance between us shortened and my eyes met hers, I sensed something was different. There was no warm smile, no step toward me, no arm around my waist—only an uncomfortable, "Hi, Chip." Before I could fully grasp what was happening, another player on our team bounced up the stairs, brushed past me, and grabbed her hand. The cold air rushed through the open

14

doors and rolled over my wet hair and numb mind. I watched in stony silence as she put her arm in his, and they walked across campus into the night. Then it hit me. She wasn't waiting for me. She was waiting for someone else. As the glass doors slowly closed behind them, I felt frozen in time.

A wave of anger swelled up from within the depths of my soul. The emotions shot through me, like pin balls bouncing indiscriminately off every object in sight. But they soon found their target. How could God let this happen to me after the great sacrifice I'd made for him? And of all the players on the team, how could God let her get hooked up with him? I knew what this guy was like. I knew his intentions with girls because of how he bragged about all his former conquests. And God had just let him walk out the door with the girl I loved?

I was livid. Worst of all, I felt betrayed. As I stood motionless in that doorway, I had a mental conversation with God: "Let's go over this one more time, God. I broke up with the beautiful girl I love, the girl I want to marry because of my commitment to you; and that snake is with her right now! You took her away from me and let her go off with him? Our relationship was the best thing you ever gave me, but I can't have it? Instead, he gets to be with her? And where is her mind? What is she doing? I don't get it!"

As I walked across campus, my fierce anger at God hardened into an attitude. I wondered whether this God I had come to know was worthy of my trust. I was seriously questioning if I wanted to continue in a relationship with a God who rewarded sacrifice and commitment with injustice and pain. This was a raw deal if ever there was one. It wasn't just about losing a girlfriend or going through the normal ups and downs of relationships in one's twenties, it was about the character of God, and whether he was trustworthy. This was personal, not just between her and me but between God and me.

I remember mumbling to myself as I made that long, lonely walk to my dorm room. "I feel like an animal. I feel like a beast. I am so angry! Why do bad people do so well? Why do people who don't walk with God get all the good stuff? And why—instead of getting good when I try to do good—why do I get what's lousy? Why is life so unfair? This stinks. God, why did you let it happen?"

Have You Ever Felt That Way?

Maybe you know exactly the kind of emotions and thoughts I'm talking about because you've had your share of them. Maybe you've experienced the pain of your mate walking out on you or the betrayal of a business partner. Perhaps you know the gnawing injustice of giving the best years of your life to your kids only to see them walk out of your life, indifferent and ungrateful for all you have done for them. Or, after you've sacrificed endless hours and significant amounts of money to care for your parents, you've felt the shock and bewilderment at being cut out of your inheritance. Perhaps you know what it's like to work harder, better, and longer in your job and then watch others get promoted because they know the boss or played the game of office politics. Maybe you, like I, have struggled to explain to your Little League son or daughter why he or she sits on the bench even though he or she is twice as good as the coach's child, who gets to play more innings. When we get a raw deal, we tend to get emotionally upset. That's where I was that night.

Okay, God, Speak to Me, Or I'm Outta Here

When I returned to my dorm room that night, I picked up my Bible and gave God an ultimatum. I had learned how to listen for God's voice as I read the Word. So I opened my Bible. I had been working my way through the Psalms. I planned to give God three, maybe four chapters. If he didn't speak to me in a way that helped me make sense of this raw deal that I'd just been handed, I was going to quit the Christian life.

To my way of thinking, God wasn't keeping up his end of the relationship. It seemed the more I committed myself to God and the more I sacrificed, the more I felt like a fool each time I got a raw deal. Tonight had been the worst. If that was the way the

Christian life was going to be, then it didn't seem worth it. I couldn't—wouldn't—worship a God like that.

I didn't grow up reading the Bible, so this was not an old habit. In fact, I didn't actually open it for the first time until I was eighteen. Yet even as a new Christian, God had spoken clearly and powerfully to me through his Word. At this point, however, I wasn't even sure if God would want to meet me in its pages—especially when I was raging at him.

How would God treat me when every fiber of my being was screaming, "God, this isn't fair"? I wasn't sure I cared. I picked up where I had left off and read the next psalm. Nothing happened. The words marched through my mind, going somewhere else. I read another psalm—nothing but empty silence. No verse jumped off the page. I began to suspect that my fears about God might prove true.

I glanced down the page to Psalm 73, and I immediately sensed something different. In the next few minutes, I had an encounter with God that has forever marked my life. He spoke to me in a way that I had never experienced before. I had no idea that the God of the universe would actually interact with a mere human in such a personal and powerful way.

I sat on my bed, tears still in my eyes, anger filling my heart, confusion clouding my soul, but as I read the psalm aloud, pausing between verses, the Spirit of God brought thoughts and pictures to my mind. It was as if I had a VCR in my head and it had just shifted from pause to play. God showed me scenes from earlier in the night and replayed the exact words I had said out loud while walking across campus. I read statements in the Scriptures almost identical to the ones I had made.

I don't want to make this sound too mystical, but God spoke to me so personally that I knew I was encountering the living God. I don't pretend that God speaks to me with such vividness on a regular basis, but I don't dare minimize this powerful event either.

Psalm 73

The following is a rendition of what occurred in my mind and heart that night as I read Psalm 73. I've placed the biblical phrases in shaded boxes, and the comments, thoughts, and pictures that came to my mind underneath them. In this way I hope you will catch a glimpse of what occurred.

> Surely God is good to Israel,
> to those who are pure in heart.
>
> verse 1

Yeah, that's what I used to believe too.

> But as for me, my feet had almost slipped;
> I had nearly lost my foothold.
> For I envied the arrogant
> when I saw the prosperity of the wicked.
>
> verses 2–3

Wow! This guy has my problem! That's exactly what just happened to me.

> They have no struggles;
> their bodies are healthy and strong.
> They are free from the burdens common to man;
> they are not plagued by human ills.
>
> verses 4–5

I nodded in agreement.

> Therefore pride is their necklace;
> they clothe themselves with violence.
> From their callous hearts comes iniquity;
> the evil conceits of their minds know no limits.
>
> verses 6–7

I thought of specific conversations I had previously had with the fellow teammate who walked off with my former girlfriend. These words described him all too well.

> They scoff.
>
> verse 8a

That summed it up, especially with that particular player. I recalled a road trip we had been on a few weeks earlier; he had scoffed and ridiculed my faith in front of other players in a hotel room.

> They scoff, and speak with malice;
> in their arrogance they threaten oppression.
> Their mouths lay claim to heaven,
> and their tongues take possession of the earth.
>
> verses 8–9

It's like that! It seems like the wicked are in control and are winning.

> Therefore their people turn to them
> and drink up waters in abundance.
>
> verse 10

The evildoers—the folks who mock God—they've got it made!

> They say, "How can God know?
> Does the Most High have knowledge?"
>
> verse 11

During conversations in the locker room, this player had said, "Oh, come on, Ingram. Get off the God stuff. You don't really believe God is in control, do you? C'mon man, you know it's all chance. Get a life. C'mon and party with us, holy man. Life is short." Reading Psalm 73 was like reading my biography!

> This is what the wicked are like—
>   always carefree, they increase in wealth.
>
> Surely in vain have I kept myself pure;
>   in vain have I washed my hands in innocence.
> All day long I have been plagued;
>   I have been punished every morning.
>
> verses 12–14

That was exactly it! My efforts to follow Jesus and live the way he wanted me to live were surely in vain. I had dated the best girl on campus. I had made a commitment before God to run our relationship his way and remain sexually pure. With that commitment came nothing but ridicule and snickers from my peers. All the other guys were out there having fun (there were four girls to every guy on our campus).

I was tied up in knots because I was trying to do what God says is right. I had more problems and frustrations as a Christian than I could ever remember having before I committed my life to Christ! But now it seemed all I had were struggles and problems. And worst of all, the greatest relationship I ever had was gone because I was following Christ. I had chosen to obey God's will for my life and in exchange had been given a raw deal!

> If I had said, "I will speak thus,"
>   I would have betrayed your children.
> When I tried to understand all this,
>   it was oppressive to me.
>
> verses 15–16

I could hardly believe another human being actually had these same thoughts. Some of the same phrases I used were right here on the page! It was almost scary! I felt goose bumps on the back of my neck as I read the line, "If I had said, 'I will speak thus,'" because it had crossed my mind what might happen if I had really told anyone the things I had muttered to myself. What if I had said that I was quitting the faith? How would that impact the six guys who were in my Bible study? I met with each of them weekly. I had the privilege of leading five of them to Christ, and they were beginning to really grow in their faith. What might happen to them if I quit the Christian faith or if they heard me talking about throwing in the towel? "God," I said, "I'm still mad at you, but I don't know that I could quit following you."

> It was oppressive to me
> till I entered the sanctuary of God;
> then I understood their final destiny.
>
> verses 16b–17

The psalmist was saying he couldn't understand the raw deals in his life. I couldn't either. Then he came before God, and he worshiped and reflected on life in light of eternity. Coming into God's presence and getting a different perspective helped him see that the wicked—those who mock God—won't get away with it forever.

My heart began to soften. My perspective began to shift. As I moved my focus off of my pain and anger, I glimpsed God's view of the whole situation.

> Surely you place them on slippery ground;
> you cast them down to ruin.
> How suddenly are they destroyed,
> completely swept away by terrors!
> As a dream when one awakes,
> so when you arise, O Lord,
> you will despise them as fantasies.
>
> verses 18–20

Yeah, there was more to life than what was going on right now. It might look like the wicked were getting a good deal and doing great—after all, that guy was out there with my girlfriend—but he was on slippery ground. How many times had I seen it happen? One day people were big stars, making all the money, proud, arrogant, mocking God, and then—boom!—God pulled the rug out from underneath them. Those people who despise God, treating him as no more than a fantasy, one day found the tables turned. The psalmist was doing the same kind of analysis I was doing in my heart at that very moment!

> When my heart was grieved
> and my spirit embittered . . .
>
> verse 21

What a descriptive phrase—and it accurately described me! How could anyone know what I was feeling? How could it be that I would be reading this particular psalm on this particular night?

> I was senseless and ignorant;
> I was a brute beast before you.
>
> verse 22

Yes, those words described me. I was so angry that I was senseless. I wasn't thinking right. I was thinking immediate cause and effect. I had even used similar words—"I'm like a beast." How could it possibly be a coincidence that the very words I spoke, and the feelings I felt, were waiting for me in my dorm room in the pages of God's Word. How else could I explain the sense that God knew I had just received an overwhelming blow to my faith?

> Yet I am always with you;
> you hold me by my right hand.
> You guide me with your counsel.
>
> verses 23–24a

22

There was my answer!

> And afterward you will take me to glory.
>
> verse 24b

I thought of all that God had done for me. I had been a Christian for only about three years, but I could see how God had guided me—even to make that difficult decision to break up, which had been a good decision in many ways. God had answered specific prayers, given me peace for the first time, and changed my life. I also knew my future was certain because of Christ's work on the cross. I was secure in the knowledge that I would spend eternity in heaven.

I realized, as I pondered this passage, that I really didn't like my life at the moment. But my present discomfort and frustration had to be viewed in light of the bigger picture that included eternity. And even though I was ticked off, I knew my relationship with God—the one I was experiencing as God met me in this very psalm—was the most real, stable, and powerful thing that had ever happened to me.

> Whom have I in heaven but you?
>
> verse 25a

I have God, I concluded, and he is for me. My relationship with that girl, a great job, friends, money, success—those things aren't secure. Those will all let me down; but God is always there for me!

As my anger subsided, I realized God alone was my security, and that security is not dependent on how I may feel at any particular moment.

> And earth has nothing I desire besides you.
>
> verse 25b

My thoughts became a halting prayer: "I hope I can say that one day, Lord, but I can't say it truthfully right now." Meanwhile, my focus was shifting from the girl I lost to the God who was there for me.

23

> My flesh and my heart may fail.
>
> verse 26a

"God, I may fail. I may blow it; in fact, I know I'll blow it."

> But God is the strength of my heart
> and my portion forever.
>
> verse 26b

The Holy Spirit seemed to have dictated this psalm specifically to help me in a way that I had never imagined possible. As I read the word "portion" in the verse above, a picture came to my mind. I thought about life being like a pie. Everyone gets a slice. I had thought that the slice that would really fulfill me was to spend my life with this girl. But God was saying directly to me, "I will be your portion, Chip. All you ever need is me. Just me, Chip; me plus nothing. It might be nice to have me plus a great job, or me plus this or that; but all you ever need to satisfy you is me. I will be your portion. I will be everything you need. I will never let you down."

As the Spirit of God spoke those words to my heart, the remaining bitterness and anger drained away. I claimed that verse—that God alone is my portion, my all sufficient helping of the pie of life. This truth has stayed with me ever since.

> Those who are far from you will perish;
> you destroy all who are unfaithful to you.
>
> verse 27

The Holy Spirit kept talking to me, reminding me, "There is a day of judgment coming. So don't live your life only for now, Chip."

> But as for me, it is good to be near God.
> I have made the Sovereign LORD my refuge;
> I will tell of all your deeds.
>
> verse 28

As the psalm ended, I realized I had done a 180-degree emotional and spiritual turnaround. I had been so mad, so embittered, so hurt. In my rage I had said to God, "If you don't speak to me tonight, I'm outta here." Even though I had not prayed reverently (and perhaps not wisely) but out of extreme anger over the raw deal I'd gotten, God heard me through my agony. And he spoke to me, clearly. I needed somewhere to turn, so I turned to this psalm, and I ended up encountering God there. Beyond just speaking to me, God went on to show me some healthy actions that I could take in response to those times when I get a raw deal.

What Raw Deal Is Eating Away at You Today?

What raw deal has happened in your life? Do you need help working through the injustice you've been handed? Are you struggling with life not being fair? Have you pushed those angry feelings so far down that you deny they even exist? Or have you already turned away from God because you have suffered wrongs, perhaps at the hands of Christians, and now you question, as I did, God's goodness, character, and faithfulness. If so, let God speak to you today through Psalm 73.

Before you read any further, let me ask you a question. What's the major raw deal in your life? Please take a moment right now to stop and think about it. I want you to read the rest of this chapter with a specific injustice in mind. I want you to bring up some of those painful memories: Who betrayed you? Who gossiped about you? Who did you in financially? Who put the screws to you? Who did something unfair to you at work? Who has talked behind your back at church? Who said things that weren't even true, but others believed them, which hurt you deeply? What happened that was out of human control but seems so unfair that you can't understand how a good God could let it happen? What happened in your life that seems completely unfair?

Let me probe a little deeper. Was your mom or dad, grandparents or siblings involved? Was your wife, husband, best friend, or one of your kids part of it? Lean back away from the page for a moment and ask God to let you face these memories—even if

25

they're painful. The more clear they become for you, the more readily God's Word will be able to reach you at your point of need.

Please take a few moments, open a Bible, and prayerfully read Psalm 73. Ask God to meet you there. Then read on to learn some of the help available in this psalm.

Experiencing God as Your Sovereign King

God is always available to us. Not only does God meet us in his Word, he wants to teach us there as well. While we experience him, he wants to equip us. He meets our needs and then prepares us for the future. The following four life lessons, drawn from Psalm 73, have been particularly helpful to me in dealing with life's raw deals.

LIFE LESSON 1: Pour Out Your Heart to God!

This is exactly what Asaph did as he wrote Psalm 73—he poured out his heart! Even godly people struggle with doubts and confusion when God's truth and their experience don't seem to match. Difficulties don't automatically mean there's something wrong with you or that you're a bad person. They can also mean that life doesn't always make sense. At times, God's truth (that God is good and in control of everything) and our experience (life stinks) don't mesh. That's what happened to me; that's what happened to Asaph; it happened to other Bible characters, and my guess is that it has probably happened to you too.

27

Asaph served as one of three directors in King David's choir. He was one of the worship leaders of the Old Testament. His writings, inspired by the Holy Spirit, made their way into the Bible and are still sung today. When his experience and God's truth didn't seem to match, this mature, godly man poured out his heart to God, which is what is preserved for us in this psalm.

Another Old Testament figure, Job, did the same thing, and he was called the most righteous man on earth. He lost his possessions, his children, and his health. He said, "God, I am angry! I don't understand what is happening or why!" In the Book of Job, chapters 29 through 31, Job wrestled with the raw deal he'd received and struggled to manage the tension of holding on to God's goodness and sovereignty while dealing with the tragic difficulties he was experiencing.

What I love about the story of Job is that God never grew angry with Job for honestly expressing his confusion, frustration, and anger. God accepted Job's hurt, pain, and everything else that overflowed from his suffering heart. Like Job, we too are welcome to tell God how much we doubt, how we sometimes wonder if he even cares. He can handle our angry accusations, our overwhelming fears, and even our blazing anger and indignation. Of course, we should remain reverent and humble enough to realize that we don't see the whole picture. But God allows us to pour out our hearts to him.

So go ahead. Allow yourself to honestly pour out your heart about the raw deals you've received. Stop keeping it all cooped up within, building layers of calluses between you and the God who loves you. God reproved Job, but he never said, "Job, don't talk to me that way." God wants us to take our anger, hurt, confusion, and doubts to him. Then he enables us to reach the point Job finally reached when he acknowledged that the working out of God's goodness and sovereignty is a mystery to us mortals. This is especially true when we get a raw deal.

Knowing that God wants us to pour out our hearts to him frees us. In fact, it may help you to know that God calls us to argue our case before him. He so longs for a relationship with us that he invites us to do so. Isaiah 43:26 says, "Put Me in remembrance, let us argue our case together, state your cause that you may be proved right" (NASB). When I was angrier with God than I had ever been in my life, when I let all my anger come fuming out honestly before God, he met me like never before. And, to my amazement, after I stated my case before him that night, he met me with compassion.

Psalm 145:18 states, "The LORD is near to all who call on him, to all who call on him in truth." That's good news only if we're willing to face the raw deal that has come our way. Could it be that you've gotten a raw deal, but you simply won't face it? Could it be that you are afraid to admit your anger openly to God? Are you afraid to acknowledge that you are angry at all? Anger is a reasonable response to injustice, especially if you have dedicated your life to a righteous and just God. So many Christians refuse to acknowledge such feelings and thoughts. Could it be that you don't want to deal with your hurt, wounds, and anger; so you keep pushing the anger back down every time it comes up? If so, realize that pent-up anger has to go somewhere. It gets planted in your body and sprouts as ulcers, headaches, bitterness, resentment, private rehearsals over the unfair situation you've endured, and outbursts of anger that are disconnected from the real source. So don't allow these raw emotions you're experiencing to fester. Instead, pour out your heart to God.

May I gently suggest that you stop reading and take a moment right now to pour out your heart to God about the specific raw deal you identified earlier in this chapter. Find a quiet place and tell God honestly how you feel. Lay it all on the table. Tell him what is really ticking you off and that you don't think it is fair. Tell him what you think, argue each point, and why you see it as you do. This is the first step toward experiencing his compassion, love, and healing from the hurt and wounds you've received. I believe that when you do, God will meet you at that point.

LIFE LESSON 2: Consider Your Choices Carefully

If you have already taken the first step and poured out your heart to God, you are ready to take step two. This is what we see

Asaph doing in Psalm 73:12–14. He stopped and carefully considered the impact his choices would have on others. You see, some of our most important decisions come when we choose *how* to respond to the raw deals we receive. Few things are as difficult to deal with emotionally and spiritually as injustice. It's at times like this that we are tempted to walk away from our faith and simply tell God it's not worth it.

So if and when you are tempted to walk away from the faith, or respond unrighteously out of anger, I urge you to carefully weigh the impact that such a decision will have on your own life and the lives of others. This was a strategic moment in Asaph's thinking, and it marked a turning point in his life. He was angry, but he realized, "If I had said, 'I will speak thus,' I would have betrayed your children" (Psalm 73:15). He realized his actions might weaken other people's faith in the Lord. You see, we never truly do anything in isolation. My actions and yours always affect the network of people around us.

As God's Spirit was walking me through Psalm 73 that remarkable evening, I imagined the six men in my college Bible study falling away from the faith when they found out that I had quit. This singular thought made me slow down and seriously weigh the possible consequences of any action I took. It is so easy to act irrationally when we are mad and hurting. Some of the dumbest things we do are done out of anger and bitterness when someone has wronged us. Every single one of us has said and done things we wished we could take back. Often these rash words and actions come out when we have been reeling from the pain of injustice.

Therefore, I implore you, as you emotionally relive the raw deal that you have faced in your life, to include this life lesson. Carefully consider, before God, all the possible implications of the actions that go through your mind. Considering the effects of such choices in the lives of others can deter us from doing anything rash that we will regret later.

Perhaps for you these words of warning come too late. Maybe you have dropped out of the faith or have become lethargic in your Christian life. Maybe you've disassociated yourself from your Bible study group or cut off a relationship in a moment of anger. It may have felt satisfying at the time, but since then that action has produced self-reproach, regret, or heartache in your life and the lives of others. Maybe these last few paragraphs have stirred up old hurts that have been living in the cellar of your soul for a long time.

You may be someone who still spends occasional time with God and are active in ministry at a superficial level, but you've never really dealt with the raw deal that he allowed into your life many years ago. You reacted on an emotional level and now you're living in the shadow of choices that you realize weren't the best for you or others. You see now the harm that has been done, but don't know how to undo it.

If this is you, God's Word to you today is that it is never too late to reconsider and take a better course of action. Life is not fair, but not dealing with what happened to you or distancing yourself from God because he allowed it to happen is not the best choice. It doesn't resolve anything, or change what happened. It doesn't remove the pain. I hope you will choose today to reconsider, because we always end up dealing with what happened to us one way or another. It's better to bring your raw deal to God and let him help you handle it.

May the Spirit of God have freedom in your heart at this moment to give you the courage to honestly examine where you're at, where you've been, and where God wants to take you. It's never too late to reconsider the impact of the decisions you've made during times when you have been wounded.

LIFE LESSON 3: See the Big Picture

The third life lesson that will help you when you've gotten a raw deal is to get a larger perspective of your situation. Get the big picture. The psalmist teaches us that we need to step into God's presence (God's sanctuary), stand in the light of truth, and regain an eternal perspective. This will allow us to look at the raw deal we're dealing with now and see what's really impor-

31

tant and what is not. We can see this happen with Asaph when he put the breaks on his downward slide. He realized that his thinking was shortsighted and temporal when it came to his evaluation of his experience.

In verse 2 Asaph says, "My feet had almost slipped"—in other words, he was ready to quit. He thought living God's way was a waste. It sounds like he was ready to give up on his relationship with God. In verse 13 he thought, "Surely in vain I have kept my heart pure." But something happened when he entered the sanctuary of God. It was then that he remembered the destiny of the wicked. In other words, in the temporal scheme of things, the wicked certainly do seem to prosper. Their way seems to be easy, while those who seek to live a righteous life by God's standards seem to have it rough. Asaph was able to get the big picture when he looked at his situation not through the lens of time, but rather from an eternal perspective.

Getting the big picture will help us endure the raw deal—the lost relationship, the lost money, the gossip, the betrayal, and the painful disappointments that come our way in this fallen world—without destroying our lives and turning us into bitter, vengeful people.

How Do We See the Big Picture?

So, practically speaking, how do you step back and see the big picture? How do you find the eternal perspective that will help you respond faithfully to a raw deal? You need some action steps that you can take no matter how you are feeling at the time. Let me offer you four key suggestions.

1. Enter the sanctuary of the Lord to worship and reflect in the light of truth.

We see that Asaph's perspective did not change until he "entered the sanctuary of the Lord." When Asaph decided to worship, his point of view shifted from a temporal to an eternal view of life. The passage doesn't tell us whether he was worshiping alone or with a congregation. But the result of entering the sanctuary of the Lord was that he started seeing life through the big lens of an eternal perspective. That made all the difference in the world.

While in the sanctuary of the Lord, Asaph's thinking was influenced by the truth God had revealed about the way things will work out in the end. He could not go into the sanctuary of the Lord without reflecting on God's character and nature. Surely he was moved by God's righteousness and promise of eventual justice and judgment against the wicked. That helped.

In light of what he knew about God's justice, Asaph took another look at the situation. He acknowledged (in verses 18–20) that life looks very good for the wicked. But he also reaffirmed the truth that no one who violates God's laws, his righteous decrees, or his authority gets by without paying a price at some point. When Asaph considered the destiny of the wicked and compared it to the destiny of the righteous, he was able to look at the present from an eternal perspective. It is this point of view that prompted the change that occurred in his heart—the same one that happened in mine.

In verses 21 and 22, Asaph says, "When my heart was grieved and my spirit embittered, I was senseless and arrogant. I was a brute beast before you." Notice the shift in verse 23 where he says, "Yet I am always with you." Like Asaph, we need to realize that regardless of what raw deals come our way, we are always with God. We always have him. We may not have the girlfriend who walked out, we may not have the inheritance, we may not have the good we deserved; yet if we have given our lives over to God, we too can say, "I am always with you, God." You can always find God, even in the midst of injustice, regardless of whatever circumstances you must temporarily endure.

As we step into the sanctuary of the Lord, we should also remember that God has all the time in the world and all eternity in which to bring about justice. Just because we have not seen the wicked punished does not mean they will get away with anything before the throne of a righteous God. If we believe that whoever has done us wrong will get away with it, the desire for vengeance and bitterness can eat us up. But if we, like Asaph, gain an eternal perspective, we can worship God now while looking forward to the time when he will bring about justice.

2. Consider how God used raw deals for good in the lives of others.

God has given us insight into how he can use what looks like a raw deal—when it's happening—to bring about good results in the long run. He has shown us this in the pages of Scripture. One classic passage is found in Genesis, chapters 37–50, where we read the story of Joseph.

Joseph was a good guy who received a bad deal. In fact, he experienced a whole series of raw deals. He was his dad's favorite, and he bragged about dreams that seemed to infer that he might be God's favorite too. So his ten brothers sold him into slavery. Even as a slave in Egypt, he did a wonderful job. He ended up in charge of the house of Potiphar, who was in Pharaoh's administration. Potiphar's wife wanted to sleep with him, but Joseph did the right thing and refused her advances. What happened? She falsely accused him of rape and he ended up in jail. While in jail, he was a great assistant to the warden; so they promoted him. Along the way he helped two fellow inmates, Pharaoh's baker and wine taster, by interpreting their dreams. As Joseph predicted, however, when the wine taster was freed from prison, he temporarily forgot Joseph back in the dungeon.

Over and over this godly man, who did what was right, received evil in return. But Joseph was persistent. There's a little phrase repeated throughout the Bible account that puts Joseph's raw deals in the right light. The phrase is "and the Lord was with Joseph." Through all of Joseph's trials, God was with him. He was with him when his brothers sold him as a slave at age seventeen. God was there every moment, through every incident of injustice, until Joseph was finally released from prison at age thirty.

As the story unfolds we can see, with the benefit of hindsight, that God had a plan he was working out all along. God's plan was to get someone in the highest position in Egypt to preserve the entire nation of Israel. He let bad things happen for a short time in order to exalt Joseph to the second highest position in the most powerful government on earth to fulfill a bigger plan.

God never lost sight of his ultimate purpose to bring about good for Joseph, and for all the Hebrew people, and ultimately for the whole world. When Joseph was finally in position and the time was right, he ended up calling all the shots, and his brothers came and bowed down to him. His entire extended family came into Egypt and were placed under his protection. They had plenty while the rest of the world went hungry. They were even given the choicest piece of land. God used Egypt as his incubator to multiply the nation of Israel to such a multitude that later the Egyptians turned on them.

Later in the story, after Joseph's father died, Joseph showed he really understood. He saw the big picture. His brothers were still uptight, and they thought, "Oh my, he's going to kill us now that Dad has died." I like to imagine Joseph leaned back with his arms crossed, looked at his brothers, and said, "You guys still don't get it, do you? You meant it for evil, but God meant it for good. God worked it all around. He used your evil intentions to accomplish a much greater good, to preserve many people" (see Genesis 50:20).

God will use your raw deal to build your character, to change your life, to give you a testimony, and to fulfill a greater purpose. But you must hang in there trusting in God to bring about a good end. The only way you can have the faith to endure events that don't make sense in the present is to shift your focus off the circumstances and back onto the big picture. Reading biblical accounts about people for whom God did this can encourage you in the meanwhile.

It also helps to consider the experiences of other people who have received a raw deal. There is a couple in our church that has been through a lot that wasn't fair, but their attitude amazes me. God used their nightmarish experiences and turned them into two stories of amazing grace. Let me briefly tell you what happened.

At age eighteen, Jerry was a college football star. One night, Jerry saw two guys fighting and tried to break it up. One of the men pulled a gun and shot Jerry at point-blank range. Jerry was paralyzed, his football career over, and his future shattered. Jerry has had to endure thirty major surgeries to deal with complications and has nearly died many times.

He described it for me, "When I first got hurt, I didn't know the Lord. I was an athlete, so I tried to get through everything by being physically and mentally tough. But the challenges became increasingly more difficult as time went on. I couldn't win on my own. Then I met Christ, and it was like the Lord jumped on the team. That made it a little bit easier. I started trusting the Lord. He got me through the times when it was hard for me to get through."

Jerry is a very tough-minded, mentally intense athlete. He is very strong-willed. His struggle, he told me, is to resist trying to do it himself and to really trust God, believing that God will turn a situation around to bring about good. When I asked Jerry to tell me exactly what good has come out of this, he said, "There's been a lot of good things. I guess the premier one is my relationship with the Lord. The second biggest is God bringing my wife, Lori, to me. She is just an incredible woman. I used to pray, 'God, if you want me to be married, bring the woman into my life you want me to be with.' When he didn't, I said, 'Okay, I guess you don't want me to have a wife.' Well, one day God did, when I met Lori here at church."

Jerry didn't just mope around, or even think to himself that he was given a raw deal. He told me, "When I got shot, I thought, 'I can't walk, but there must be something I can do.' I just didn't know what it was going to be. With God's help, I eventually found many things I can do."

Jerry played on the U.S. Olympic wheelchair basketball team and won a gold medal. He's a world-class wheelchair marathoner and has traveled all over the world, both in competition and as a missionary. He teamed up with Joni Eareckson Tada and shared how Christ took his bad situation and turned it around for good.

He recounted one moment when he was on the starting line in the Olympic Games in the fifteen hundred meters. "The final event in the pentathlon (a competition that combines five events) was about to begin when I looked up and saw myself on the big screen with my name there to show that I was representing the United States. I thought, "Wow. This is really cool. Thank you, Lord. It doesn't get much better than this!"

I asked Jerry how he keeps going, even with all the physical challenges he faces every day. He gave me this example. "Let's say

I had a really hard marathon, which is twenty-six miles, but I knew at the beginning of the race that no matter what happened, I was guaranteed to win. So no matter how bad the hills were, or whether there was a crash, or how tired I got, I would win. Would I enter the race? Of course. So would you. It's the same idea in my relationship with the Lord. I have an advantage. I read the end of the book and I know the end of the story. We win. I know there will be an eternity where I will not be hampered like I am here. So it doesn't matter what I have to go through here. I'm looking forward to the finish line and the medal ceremony."

The story of Jerry's wife, Lori, is just as inspiring. Lori was raped and beaten while serving in the military as a young woman. I can imagine few things in all of life as crushing and unjust as what Lori experienced. In the aftermath of the trauma, she endured a ten-year relationship in which she and her daughter were emotionally and physically abused. She's had twenty-three major surgeries in the last few years to deal with her physical problems, but she too lives with a positive outlook and an eternal perspective.

Lori says she couldn't have survived without God's presence in her life. She says of Jerry, "God has blessed me with somebody who understands the kinds of challenges I face. God has given me support through Jerry and through friends who are there for me and who don't hesitate to stop and talk." When I asked Lori what she does when it's one of those days and she has thoughts like, "I can't go through one more surgery. There are too many hassles. There's too much pain," she said she turns to God in prayer and to her friends.

She also relies on certain promises God gives in the Bible. One of them is, "'For I know the plans I have for you,' declares the LORD, 'plans to prosper you and not to harm you, plans to give you hope and a future. Then you will call upon me and come and pray to me, and I will listen to you. You will seek me and find me when you seek me with all your heart'" (Jer. 29:11–12). Even though she has endured terrible injustice and pain inflicted on her wrongfully, Lori knows there is a God who has good plans for her. As she calls on him and seeks him, she is confident that God will be there for her and lead her to the fulfillment of the good plans he has for her.

She goes on to say, "If I had to do it over again, I don't think I would change it because I wouldn't be the person I am today without the trials and the struggles—and I do mean struggles—I had to go through and still do. God took two people who had a really rough time and put us together as a team. Now we can go out and speak to just about anybody. Because of all we've been through, we have some inkling of what has happened to others. We can let them know that God can turn it all around. Whether you have been attacked or you've been abused or you were a victim of violence, God is faithful. He will carry you through it. He will take your hand. He will walk with you there. But there is a process you have to go through and you have to trust him. Don't just look at the circumstances. Circumstances are like quicksand; I'd drown in them in a heartbeat. But if you look at God and keep that eternal perspective, keep your eyes on him, not on yourself or what anybody else thinks, he will lift you up."

I certainly can't improve on Lori's statement!

3. Talk with those who can help you see things from God's perspective.

It's easy to get so close to a situation we're in that we have a hard time seeing clearly. Sometimes we can't seem to get our eyes off all the minute details of who did us wrong and what happened. At times like this I try to get around people who have lived decades longer than I, have walked with God longer, and know God much more intimately. Sometimes, talking over what you are thinking with someone who can look at your situation objectively and analyze it from a biblical perspective can help you broaden your outlook.

I can't tell you how much the community of believers of which I'm a member has meant to me in coping with some raw deals that have come my way. Once my character was attacked and my name slandered. It touched my pride so deeply that I had a deep emotional block in attempting to work through this issue. Everything in me wanted to get back at these people who attacked me. I needed close friends who would listen, care, pray, and (of vital importance) point me to God's Word as I tried to see what I should do.

I remember a lunch with a fellow pastor when I was in the midst of one of my major self-pity parties. I was in the process of rationalizing, in a very sophisticated way, how to get back at the person who had attacked me. In a gentle voice, he said, "I sense you're still pretty angry about this."

I brushed him off and said, "No, it's not about anger. This is about bringing about God's justice and helping the kingdom of God grow. Justice needs to happen here!"

He opened his Bible and read these verses to me, "But how is it to your credit if you receive a beating for doing wrong and endure it? But if you suffer for doing good and you endure it, this is commendable before God. To this you were called, because Christ suffered for you, leaving you an example, that you should follow in his steps" (1 Peter 2:20–21). Then he looked me in the eye and said, "Chip, I think God wants you to suffer for doing what is right. Don't strike back. Don't retaliate. Let God work his way in this situation."

I had been on the verge of writing a letter and making a few phone calls that would have been pretty stupid and potentially harmful. I was so close to the situation, so consumed with how it had hurt me that I hadn't viewed my situation through the applicable biblical truth that my friend shared with me. God protected me from myself through the wise counsel of a brother who cared enough to speak the truth in love. By giving me his biblical perspective, he helped me see the big picture when I could barely see past my own pain and pride.

When you lose sight of the big picture, get together with people who know you best, love you most, and who know God's Word well enough to help you find truth that applies to what you are going through.

4. Look at life through the binoculars of God's goodness and sovereignty.

To bounce back from injustice you might need spiritual binoculars. Binoculars have two lenses that you look through simultaneously in order to see farther and more clearly. To get the big picture, and therefore to be able to endure whatever raw deals you get in this life, I suggest that you learn to look at life through the lenses of God's goodness and sovereignty.

To help you do this, I recommend A. W. Tozer's book *The Knowledge of the Holy*. By studying this book, you'll learn in a powerful way that God's goodness requires that justice will prevail in the end. In other words, God, who is innately good, will not let the bad guys win. God is sovereign, which means he is the rightful ruler over all that is; God is the king of the world. And because God is king, he is also in control. He allows whatever happens to us, and he will work it ultimately for our good. God didn't get caught off guard when that person walked out of your life or when your partner changed the books and put the screws to you. God wasn't saying, "Oh my gosh, what happened over there?" He's aware of it and he's in control and he's just. He will deal justly with that person who treated you unjustly. He will work it around, ultimately, for your good if you don't bail out of the process.

This truth is simply put in this New Testament promise: "And we know that in all things God works for the good of those who love him, who have been called according to his purpose" (Rom. 8:28). God is working out a larger plan for your life than you can imagine. God has better intentions for you than you have for yourself. And he knows that you live in a world where forces of evil work against the good he has planned for you. But if you love God and put your trust in him and if you set your life in keeping with his purpose for you, he promises to cause all things—even the times when you get a raw deal—to work together for your good. This does not mean all that happens to you will be good. Rather, it means God will work all things together to accomplish good for you ultimately. When you can look at your life simultaneously through faith that God is good and God is sovereign, you will be able to keep the bigger picture in sight.

LIFE LESSON 4: Reaffirm Your Relationship with God

We've been focusing on Asaph when he was pouring out his heart to God. Eventually Asaph was able to move from his emotions to a logical evaluation as he carefully considered his choices and the impact they might have on others. In the beginning of the psalm, we see him despairing because he is getting a raw deal while the wicked prosper, but this is only until he enters the sanctuary of the Lord.

When he begins to see present injustices in light of coming judgment and in light of all eternity, his heart begins to change. In the end he comes around to the point where he sees God in heaven and says, "Whom have I in heaven but you? And earth has nothing I desire besides you" (v. 25).

We see a major shift in Asaph's thinking when he moves from processing his difficult situation to focusing his heart on the person of God. That's when he reaffirms his relationship with God by saying, "My flesh and my heart may fail, but God is the strength of my heart and my portion forever" (v. 26). When we come to verse 28, Asaph says, "But as for me, it is good to be near God. I have made the Sovereign LORD my refuge; I will tell of all your deeds."

Even though he started out struggling with the feeling that he was getting a raw deal, he eventually realized that he was getting a great deal—a personal and eternal relationship with the living God.

By the end of Psalm 73, Asaph is no longer fuming about getting a raw deal. He realizes that heaven is waiting for him. The Sovereign Lord, who reigns from heaven, has everything under control; the wicked will pay for their wrongdoing, and God will ultimately work everything out for Asaph's good. That really doesn't sound like a raw deal after all, does it?

God wants to do the same thing with you. God wants to take the worst things that come your way and use them for your good! At one point, when I was talking to Jerry, the man whose story I shared earlier, I asked him, "Jerry, what difference has your relationship with Christ made in terms of how you deal with the raw deals you've received?"

He grinned mischievously and said, "What makes you think I got a raw deal?"

LIFE LESSONS TO APPLY

1. Pour out your heart to God.

2. Carefully consider your choices and their potential impact on others.

3. Get the big picture (the eternal perspective that God will bring about justice).

   ✓ Enter the sanctuary of the Lord to worship and reflect in the light of truth.
   ✓ Consider how God used raw deals for good in the lives of others.
   ✓ Talk with those who can help you see things from God's perspective.
   ✓ Look at life through the binoculars of God's goodness and sovereignty.

4. Reaffirm your relationship with God.

EXPERIENCING GOD WHEN YOU GET A RAW DEAL

Somewhere you can turn: Psalm 73

KEY VERSE

But as for me, it is good to be near God.
I have made the Sovereign Lord my refuge.

Psalm 73:28a

2

I am with you . . .

IN TIMES
OF CRISIS

In Chinese the word "crisis" is written with two distinct characters. One pictograph can mean either "tragedy" or "danger." The other means "opportunity." The eastern mind thinks of a crisis as either a great opportunity or a great tragedy. We are about to look at the kind of crisis that emphasizes opportunity. Danger or tragedy might be around the next corner, but the moment is filled with a kind of anxiety that may be the prelude to something wonderful or something terrible. We just don't know yet. We do know that the choices and decisions we make will influence the outcome. The specific kind of crisis I have in mind results from major transitions, when life demands that we leave the past behind and move on to new pastures.

The Beginnings of a Crisis

I've had a number of crises in my life. I admit I haven't struggled nearly as much as others have, but my crises have certainly been hard enough for me. Like any other family, we've had health issues, tragedies, struggles, and tensions. We've had unexpected circumstances, overwhelming pressures, and family situations when we wondered how in the world we would ever make it. One of the most difficult crises I've ever gone through was the prelude to the biggest decision of my life.

I was twenty-three years old and ready to be married. I had met a beautiful, godly woman who had been through a lot of difficulty. She knew God like few women I'd ever known and had a passion to serve and follow Christ. In many ways, we seemed to be designed for each other! But there were complications.

When I first met Theresa, she was working at a college in West Virginia. I had gone there to look for a job. I was already leading a ministry on the campus, and I thought having a job at the school would help to make ends meet and provide a greater platform for ministry. We soon discovered we were both Christians, and she later attended a large Bible study I was leading. Within a couple of weeks, she came to the Bible study with two small twin boys. They were as cute as they could be, not much over two years old. I still remember the blue pajamas with the zippers up the front—you know, the kind little kids wear that have the feet in them. I also thought it was a shade inappropriate to bring these two small children that she was baby-sitting to a group made up primarily of college and early-career students. But she was young in the faith and it was understandable.

Only later did I learn she wasn't baby-sitting. The twins were hers. She brought them on purpose, so I would know she had two children. When I found that out, my heart sank. I had no idea that she was already a mother. Although I longed to build a deeper relationship with her, this put a stop sign right there at the fork in the road. I shifted emotionally and began to resist any romantic thoughts. I decided to become her friend and to hope that God would provide a husband for her sometime in the future. I knew I wanted to be married some day soon, but I was far from being ready to be a father.

The Plot Thickens

The story I could tell is long and involved, but I will try to condense it for you. Theresa and I became very good friends over the next year. I struggled to keep my defenses up. She secretly prayed and believed that I might well be her future husband and father to her children. You have to remember that this was in the mid-1970s and the church was having a difficult time dealing with the rapid changes in the culture. The church's response to sin tended to emphasize legalism and judgment rather than mercy and forgiveness.

I soon learned more about Theresa's background. She had gone through a devastating divorce prior to becoming a Christian. Her husband had abandoned her shortly after the twins were born. She eventually discovered her husband had been involved with another woman for well over a year prior to the birth of the boys. The marriage ended and her life was shattered.

In her desperation and pain, she sought answers but could find none. At her lowest point, when she thought there was no hope or reason for living, she had a conversation with her boss at the college. God moved him to communicate what it meant to have a relationship with Christ. Theresa learned that God loved her and had a plan for her and her boys. Just when she had run out of places to look for answers, God met her in a tiny church outside Fairmont, West Virginia. She trusted in Christ and began a journey with a group of women who were focused on intercessory prayer and learning to hear God's voice.

For the first two years of her new faith, she didn't know much, except that God loved her and that when she talked with him, he listened. She saw miracle after miracle as he provided for her and her two young children. She then began to pray that God would bring a man into her life. Because she wanted to say thanks to God by giving her life in full-time service to him, she prayed that he would be a pastor.

At the time I had no real desire to be a pastor. In fact, it never entered my mind. But after doing college ministry for several years, I did believe God wanted me to be a missionary. After some graduate work and further ministry on college campuses, I determined that my life direction was going to be missions.

Unexpected Turn

Meanwhile, our friendship grew. I thought I had avoided any possible romantic dangers. In fact, I vividly remember praying that God would bring a godly man into Theresa's life. I had no idea I might be that man. Then in a most amazing way, while three thousand miles away from Theresa, I suddenly fell in love with her.

I was traveling as part of an evangelistic basketball team in Caracas, Venezuela. During a time of prayer, God unexpectedly brought Theresa to my mind. I realized for the first time that I might well

47

be the answer to her prayer, and she might be the answer to mine. After I returned home, we began dating. Very cautiously, I got to know the boys more personally. Theresa and I made sure that we did nothing more than hold hands, as I was very fearful about the implications of our relationship on me, on her, and on the future of these young boys.

By this point, I knew that God wanted me in full-time ministry, but I was getting conflicting relationship advice from those I respected most. Many told me that God would never use my life if I married a divorced woman. Others said the Bible was very clear that when a person has a divorce prior to their conversion or has been abandoned by an unbelieving mate, God not only forgives but also restores and allows that person to remarry. I had been a Christian for only about five years and was no biblical expert. Conflicting voices and shifting emotions made my life miserable. More and more I realized that I was drawn to Theresa and wanted to spend the rest of my life with her. But voices I trusted were cautioning that might not be the will of God. And yet, we could not simply stay in limbo.

The crisis was real. As the Chinese made clear by their pictographs for "crisis," I faced both a great opportunity and a possible tragedy. It was the most difficult decision I ever had to make, and I didn't make it quickly. Months and months dragged on as our relationship continued to develop. Theresa and the boys were a wonderful part of my life. But I wasn't sure they were meant to be in my future. I felt my emotions and thoughts go up and down like a yo-yo. We sought God together and I asked him to show us his will. I fasted for two, three, four days at a time. I got counsel from everyone I knew. I read every book on divorce and remarriage I could find and studied every Bible passage. For months, I agonized on the sharp edge of indecision.

A Step Back

No one asks for crises. They simply come with the changes that regularly occur in a fallen world. I'm not talking about predicaments where we are stuck in difficult circumstances that we can't escape. That's what we will look at in the chapter on being gripped by fear (chapter 5). In this chapter we will look at *going through* the kinds of crises in which life moves on, and we must move on also. Something that was satisfying and secure one day is gone. One epoch of life is over and we must embark upon the next. Moving forward is our only option. The question of how to move forward creates the crisis.

Sometimes these life changes appear positive, like graduating from college or beginning a new career. Other times the transitions seem oppressively negative, like adjusting to the loss of a job or the sudden death of a spouse.

Whether the crisis comes in our relationships, families, careers, health, finances, or in other aspects of life, such moments are actually full of opportunities. We hesitate to move on, but we can't stay where we are, doing what we've been doing. These times of transition are dangerous because one wrong move, one faulty decision, one misstep could have far-reaching consequences. Meanwhile, good decisions, smart moves, and courageous steps in the right direction hold the promise of future blessings. There's a lot at stake.

During such times we need more than the resolve to move forward without looking back. We need someone to lead us, someone to provide for us and protect us, someone to tell us what we should do, someone to guide us safely through. At such times we need to encounter God as our shepherd. With that in mind, we will look at the Twenty-third Psalm.

Before we look at this familiar psalm, I want you to imagine a white-board in your mind. Pull out an imaginary marker, and then ask yourself, "If I had to jot down one major life transition now looming before me that creates a crisis for me, what would it be?" If you're not currently facing such a change, ask yourself, "What kind of change would create an immediate crisis for me?"

Perhaps it's the possibility of losing your job. Maybe you're wondering how you will go on when you're an adult, no longer dependent on your parents. Maybe you're wondering how you'd move on after a breakup with a girlfriend or boyfriend. Perhaps it's deciding what college to attend, whom to marry, which job offer to accept, or where to move. Maybe it has to do with a transition into retirement, adjusting to parenthood, going through an unwanted divorce, or dealing with the death of a spouse. Perhaps your financial situation is precarious and you don't know what to do.

The scenarios above are external. What about the crises in your hidden life? Maybe it's a change you know you have to make for your own well-being, but it's hard, like giving up a bad habit or diverting yourself from an area of sin that you finally realize is destroying you from the inside out.

All such changes and life transitions—whether foisted upon you by circumstances or created by a realization that you need to change in order to survive—create a type of crisis. They demand that you do something. You can't just sit still and see what happens. Life is moving on and so must you. The question is not, *will* we go through such times of transition and crisis. The question is, *how* will we go through them and to what end.

Will we go through them alone? Will we keep a stiff upper lip? Will we be crushed under the weight of our decisions? Will we collapse in despair or lapse into denial? Will the results leave us bitter, resentful, and inwardly focused? Will we stumble off into sin, cower in fear, or cautiously move ahead with courage and hope? Will we go through times of crisis in such a way that we will know God better? Will we experience his presence, his power to protect us, and the comfort of his Word to guide us faithfully through? Will we end up being destroyed in the dangers and overtaken by tragedy, or will we come out the other end to a better life, as better people, more Christ-like, and stronger?

During those months of agonizing over the decision concerning Theresa, thoughts raced back and forth through my mind. The usual people I loved the most had given me conflicting counsel. They all cared about me, but they all had very different ideas about what was best for my life. They disagreed on what the Bible taught, and was uncertain about the most important decision of my life.

What I needed most of all was a shepherd. I needed someone to lead me and guide me and help me understand what God wanted for my life in a way I could understand. I needed to encounter God in this time of crisis. I needed to have him lead me through to the green pastures and still waters that would satisfy my deepest needs.

You may find yourself in a crisis or a transition similar to mine, or far different, but we all need a shepherd to lead us through such uncertain times. As I sought to follow God while deciding whether or not to marry Theresa, I learned some lifelong lessons that transformed my relationship with God. I discovered that all the voices in the world could never replace the voice of the Good Shepherd. I learned that God would indeed lead and guide me in paths of righteousness. I learned that he is good and that if I would learn to listen to his voice, he would clearly lead me—not around the crisis, but right through it.

In the end, though it was really a beginning, God led me to marry Theresa. I have never had any regret over that decision. I also am grateful for what I learned of God's leading in the process. As we look at Psalm 23 together, my prayer for you is that you will encounter God in a way that will allow you to experience him as your shepherd when you go through times of transition and crisis.

PSALM 23

The shepherd's psalm is perhaps one of the better-known passages of literature in the world. Its comforting words are read at most funerals. The familiar phrases are memorized by Sunday school children. Even people who are unfamiliar with the Bible seem to know about the "valley of the shadow of death," and they can finish the phrase, "The Lord is my ____." It's the Twenty-third Psalm. But before we look at it, please do me one favor, okay? Don't get into that "Oh, isn't it beautiful. What nice poetry" mindset. Since the words are so familiar, you may just nod your head and say, "Oh, yes. The Lord is my shepherd." You recognize the words, but do you understand their truth? God can be your shepherd, but what does that mean?

In order to understand this psalm, we need to consider it in the historical context in which it was written. Since most of us aren't shepherds and don't know a whole lot about sheep, we can miss a great deal of the meaning. This psalm is more than a beautiful poem. When God inspired David, by the Holy Spirit, to write Psalm 23, he used words and pictures that made great sense to his contemporary Hebrews. Once we understand those ideas, they can instruct us the same way today. Let me give you a little background on sheep and shepherds, so that as you read this passage, you can grasp the full impact of what it means for Christ to be your shepherd in your time of crisis.

Psalm 23 reads:

> The LORD is my shepherd, I shall not be in want.
> He makes me lie down in green pastures,
> he leads me beside quiet waters,
> he restores my soul.
> He guides me in paths of righteousness
> for his name's sake.
> Even though I walk
> through the valley of the shadow of death,
> I will fear no evil,
> for you are with me;
> your rod and your staff,
> they comfort me.
>
> You prepare a table before me
> in the presence of my enemies.
> You anoint my head with oil;
> my cup overflows.
> Surely goodness and love will follow me
> all the days of my life,
> and I will dwell in the house of the LORD
> forever.

Notice the first line. It says, "The LORD is my shepherd." The Bible includes many names for God. This title, "LORD," means Yahweh or Jehovah, God's great covenant name. This is the name by which he revealed himself to Abraham. Literally it means "I am that I am." It refers to God's transcendence, his eternal otherness. The word expresses the most comprehensive picture of God that can fill our minds. When we say "Lord" in the sense of "Yahweh," we are echoing back what only God can truly say: "*I am* before all else. *I am* self-existent. *I am* self-sufficient. *I am* holy. *I am* above. *I am* unlimited in power and resources. *I am* outside of time. *I am* eternal. Yahweh, the great *I AM!*" Then in a voice that calls out to our deepest longings, the Lord whispers, "I am your shepherd."

This entire psalm expresses a metaphor—sheep and a shepherd. I wonder how many people reading this book have ever herded sheep or have looked at life from a sheep's perspective.

53

Not many, I'm sure. This metaphor, however, casts us as sheep. In fact, the Bible refers to believers over two hundred times as sheep. Unfortunately for most of us, our last close and personal encounter with sheep was likely at a petting zoo. Translation? We don't know much about sheep.

By contrast, when Hebrews heard this psalm for the first time three thousand years ago, the words connected and pictures came to mind. They grasped a new understanding about God. They learned about the intimacy God desires to have with his people. And they were introduced to a concept that would later be fully revealed by a man who said, "I am the good shepherd" (John 10:11). We can't grasp this same understanding unless we get a clearer picture of sheep and shepherds.

A Closer Look at Sheep

Sheep have some interesting characteristics. Don't take this too personally, but sheep are among the densest animals God made. Sheep are slow and easily frightened. They are defenseless by nature. When sheep are in danger, they don't growl or fight back. Their wilderness skills don't add up to much. In fact, the equation apart from a good shepherd looks something like this: danger + sheep = death. Sheep are not very clean, unlike cats. Some people don't like cats, but at least they're clean. Cats lick themselves all the time. Sheep are dirty and smelly; they pick up parasites easily. Sheep cannot find food or water without help. Every deer knows where to find food; even rabbits can locate water. Animals for the most part have keen survival skills—not sheep. Left alone, sheep will stay in one place, eat the grass down to the roots, and ruin the land. Unless someone leads them to green pastures, they'll stay there on the barren land and bleat until they die. Sheep are so easily frightened that if a cool stream bubbles and splashes too much, they will not approach to get life-giving water because they're afraid of the sound. That's why a good shepherd will often dam up a stream and create a pool or a quiet place where the flock will not be afraid to get a drink.

A Closer Look at Hebrew Shepherds

Now before you get a little defensive, thinking, "Now that I know more about sheep I'm a little offended that the Bible refers to me like that," bear in mind how God cast himself in this metaphor. The shepherd was the lowliest job on the Hebrew social scale. Growing up in my house, the lowest job was taking out the garbage. That's the job that always got bumped down to the youngest kid. When you were in a Hebrew family, the lowest job was watching the sheep. You had to stay with them, provide for their needs, protect them, and lead them. David, the youngest son of Jesse of Bethlehem, who became king of Israel and wrote Psalm 23, knew first hand about shepherding.

The Shepherd's Equipment

Every shepherd's equipment included a rod and staff. The rod was a long, strong stick with a knob on the end. The rod was being carried in the belt and used to kill wild animals that would come around seeking a sheep to devour. A good shepherd could throw that rod with such precise aim and deadly force that he could protect the sheep from the predators. His other piece of equipment was a staff. You know, the tall pole with a crook at the top. You've seen it in Christmas card pictures and classic paintings of the Good Shepherd. Even Little Bo Peep carries a staff in nursery-rhyme illustrations. The shepherd's staff had many uses, but most of them involved keeping the sheep on the right path and out of trouble. The sheep, being clueless, regularly wandered off and got into thorn bushes. The crook of the staff was used to pull them out. When they strayed too close to the edge and fell into ravines, the shepherd used the crook of the staff to lift them up and pull them out. When the shepherd saw a sheep beginning to stray into dangerous territory, now and then he'd use the staff to give them a little rap on their rear end as if to say, "Hey, we're not doing that." So the rod served as an instrument of protection from predators, while the staff kept the sheep on the right paths or rescued them

55

when they got off into dangerous territory. A good shepherd knew how to use both the rod and the staff.

An Intimate Relationship between Sheep and Shepherd

Notice that the psalm does not say, "The Lord is *the* shepherd." It says, "The Lord is *my* shepherd." As more than one writer has pointed out, this may be the most intimate, personal term ever given to God in the Old Testament. The Hebrew mind had been trained to resist casual references to God. They didn't even write out God's name because they wanted to show respect. So the opening words of this psalm may have shocked them before it comforted them.

They understood the kind of relationship a good shepherd has with each of his sheep. He stays with them, night and day, often sleeping at the doorway to the sheepfold, putting his own body between the sheep and any predator. He provides for, protects, cares for, understands, nourishes, and loves his sheep. He knows each ewe and ram by name. Each sheep must depend completely on its shepherd for life, but the shepherd also loves his sheep and is willing to risk his life to preserve theirs. This psalm took a familiar setting and applied it unexpectedly to a divine relationship.

Even though being a shepherd was a lowly job, a serving job, it was also a vital job. In the first line we see God's transcendence, his bigness, his greatness, his power as *I Am*, Jehovah. And yet, alongside this, we see him being called "my shepherd," which shows us God's imminence, his tenderness, and his personal relationship to each sheep. Take special note of the pronoun "my." You might want to circle all the first-person pronouns in this psalm, "my," "I," and "me." David wasn't writing about a distant God. David knew a God who intimately cares about all his sheep.

To the ancient Hebrew, sheep were vulnerable, but they were also valuable. How was a Hebrew home sustained? What did they eat? They ate mutton, leg of lamb, and lamb chops. How did they make money? They sheared the sheep. One reason shepherds counted sheep was because they were the equivalent of a bank account! In spite of their obvious deficiencies, sheep were highly valued among God's people.

Juxtaposed with God's almighty transcendence, we are as fragile as sheep. Compared to God's divine wisdom, we're as clueless as sheep. Judged by our decisions and living, we're as prone to wander and stray as sheep. We're as vulnerable to sin as a sheep is to falling into a ravine. According to God's Word, however, he considers us extraordinarily valuable and worthy of his protection.

Once David sets up the metaphor of God the shepherd, he shows us his unshakable confidence in God, regardless of what shadowy valleys he would have to pass through in life. Reading through the psalm we can clearly see what gave David such confidence and how we can gain it for ourselves for when God leads us through our times of crisis.

David's Secrets to Confidence in Times of Crisis

This psalm includes three statements in the future tense. Everything else is in the present tense. Consider them.

"I *shall not* be in want."
"I *will* fear no evil."
"I *will* dwell in the house of the Lord forever."

David had been through enough to understand who God is. He had been in danger as a shepherd boy, a young soldier, and a fugitive. He had been through dangerous transitions when there was no telling how things would turn out. He knew all about crises. Somewhere along the line, the Spirit of God revealed to David the secret of having unshakable confidence, even while taking steps forward in uncertain circumstances. The more David's life and the survival of his fellows hung in the balance, the closer he walked with God.

This is the kind of confidence that can help when someone has cancer and has to decide whether to take the chemotherapy or go another way. How else can someone in that situation say, "I will fear no evil"? It's the kind of confidence that comes when you have to decide from a position of godly stewardship whether to take your money out of the market or let it ride. When your finances are uncertain and you have to decide what to do, can you say, "I shall not be in want"? When you stare into eternity at the end of your life, can you say, "I will dwell in the house of the LORD forever"? This psalm can give us that kind of confidence in God no matter what uncertainties we face or life-or-death decisions we must make.

Now let's look at this psalm and discover David's secrets. How could he speak about God in this way? What did he know? It's all there in Psalm 23. In the first statement of absolute confidence he says, "I shall not be in want." Why? Because the shepherd provided for all his needs. That was the key. David had decided, "I'm not going to be uptight. I know I will not be in want because the shepherd, *my* shepherd, the all-knowing, the all-powerful shepherd, God, will provide. He's going to take care of all my needs."

God Has You Covered: Physically, Emotionally, and Spiritually

Three key areas of personal need underlie David's words: physical, psychological/emotional, and spiritual. He reminds us that the Almighty God of the universe is committed to meeting our physical, emotional, and spiritual needs.

When David wrote, "He makes me lie down in green pastures," he knew that sheep don't look for the best grass on their own. The shepherd *makes* them go to where they can get their physical needs met. Likewise, God will take you to places where you will be physically nourished. When it says, "He leads me beside quiet waters," it speaks of taking care of the sheep's physical needs. Sheep will not lie down in grass, graze freely, or drink from the still waters if there is friction within the flock, danger lurking outside of the flock, or if there are parasites within their bodies. In other words, their physical needs have to be met before they can lie down.

58

One word of caution is in order here. God doesn't promise to meet your wants, and he doesn't necessarily follow your agendas. The promises of provision and protection stand as long as we follow and trust. When we are going through times of decision and major life transitions, we certainly should ask God to give us the desires of our hearts, understanding that he will lead us to that which is best. Sometimes that may be just what we were hoping for, as when I sought God about whether or not I should marry Theresa. Sometimes God will answer in miraculous ways. Sometimes, however, God will take us through situations we never would choose for ourselves and allow us to deal with dangerous times of following him through "the valley of the shadow of death." Whatever the circumstances, we can experience God's provision, protection, and guidance. He promises to lead us to a place where there are green pastures and quiet waters.

As we follow God through such times of transition, we can trust that he will provide not only sustenance for our physical body but also restoration for our souls. The word "restore" literally means "to repent" or "to be converted." There will be times when God will actually allow a crisis in order to get us to change or turn around and follow *his* agenda. When the ancient Hebrews used the term "soul," they were referring to the whole person or the self. So the idea here is that God restores us to wholeness. He takes our deepest needs and our deepest hurts, puts us on the right path, and restores us. He puts us back together. And while he's giving us his grace, turning us around, pulling us out of trouble, he's ministering to our whole being.

But that's not all. The psalm goes on to indicate what God seeks to do through us. God's purpose is not only to make us whole but also to lead us into a life that speaks to others for him. We can have confidence, like David, that God will guide us, give us direction, and show us how to walk "in paths of righteousness" or literally "the right path."

When you and I have to move forward and make important, life-changing decisions, how do we know what to choose? What's right? What's wrong? What's true? Whom should we marry? What job should we take? Should we get involved in this or not? That's when you and I need to claim God's promise that he will lead and direct us as clearly as he did David. Note: He leads us in the right path for "his name's sake." God is more committed to revealing his will to us than we are to following it. I assure you that if you will come to the place where you are honestly willing to do whatever God directs you to do, he will show you what to do one hundred percent of the time (Ps. 32:8).

All the elements of David's metaphor blend together. Lush green pastures and quiet waters supply the physical aspects of the picture. Then comes the restoring of the soul, where the good shepherd takes care of our psychological or emotional needs. The picture is complete as he leads us in paths of righteousness, for this is the spiritual aspect of our need. The three parts of the picture don't function separately. They blend together. In ways we can't fathom, God orchestrates people and circumstances all around us to meet our physical, emotional, and spiritual needs. David, speaking from the sheep's point of view, is confident that God will meet all his needs. And we can be confident that he'll meet all our needs too.

The Valley of the Shadow of Death

The little phrase "the valley of the shadow of death" describes a frequent event in the physical life of the sheep. During part of the year, the shepherd keeps his flock in the lowlands, where the grazing is good. When the weather changes and all the lush grass is up in the mountains, the shepherd leads his sheep through ravines and valleys to get to green pastures. So, in the course of changing seasons, the flock must journey through the mountains, in and out of darkness in the "valleys of shadows."

Those shadowy valleys are where the predators lie in wait to capture their prey. As sheep go through the darkness, they can't see the predators. A lion or wolf could come out, snatch a sheep, and kill it before a lax shepherd would know anything about it. When the sheep go through those valleys, they sense the danger. They know fear.

That's the scene David described. Literally, "the valley of the shadow of death" refers to the flock's travels through unfamiliar

60

and dangerous territory; figuratively, it relates to those dark times when you cannot make sense of what is going on around you. The promise here isn't simply that God will take us through the shadow of the fear of death, but that he will takes us through whatever crisis we face, no matter how fearful or dangerous. David assures us that we don't have to be afraid because God is with us, even when we go through such valleys.

Phillip Keller wrote an excellent book called *A Shepherd Looks at Psalm 23* that gives further insight on this psalm. He was a sheep-herder for many years in Australia. He devoted an entire chapter to the valley of the shadow. He wrote, "The shepherd knows from past experience that predators like coyotes, bears, wolves or cougars can take cover in these broken cliffs and from their vantage point prey on his flock. He knows these valleys can be subject to sudden storms and flash floods that send walls of water rampaging down the slopes. There could be rockslides, mud, or snow avalanches and a dozen other natural disasters that would destroy or injure his sheep. But in spite of such hazards he also knows that this is still the best way to take his flock to the high country. He spares himself no pains or trouble or time to keep an eye out for any danger that might develop."[1]

When David wrote, "Even though I walk through the valley of the shadow of death, I will fear no evil," he was making a radical statement. He declared that he knew how dangerous this fallen world could be, but he refused to give in to fear. How could he express such confidence? David simply and boldly trusted God as his shepherd to guard him against all natural disaster, all enemies, and all predators. Note that he even cited three reasons that can give us the same kind of confidence when we go through such dangerous valleys: (1) "For you are *with me*," (2) "your *rod*," (3) "and your *staff*, they comfort me." Let's look at each of these.

God's Presence Equals Provision and Protection

The first reason we don't have to be afraid in the midst of crisis is because God will go through it with us. Whatever your crisis may be, whenever the darkness of your valley obscures your view of the future, whatever predators or enemies may be laying in wait, God promises, "I will be with you." Hebrews 13:5b and 6 confirms this promise, "For He Himself has said, 'I will never desert you; nor will I ever forsake you,' so that we confidently say, 'The Lord is my helper; I will not be afraid. What will man do to me?'" (NASB). God is saying, "I will always be with you and never ever leave you or forsake you." He could hardly say it any stronger. I don't understand how it works. All I know is that in the worst and most difficult times, when we come to the end of ourselves, God's presence invisibly travels those dark valleys with us.

As a pastor, I've been with people during some of the darkest times they will ever face. I've sat next to believers in the intensive care unit after an accident has claimed their child or cancer has consumed their mate. I've stood by a brother in the smoke and dust after his business literally went up in flames. As hard as some of these moments have been, they have given me a priceless front-row seat as I watch in amazement as God's gracious, empowering presence has surrounded and supported those who have lost so much. I have seen God literally carry these people along in a transparent, protective bubble through the harshest and most painful early days. I cannot deny his presence.

When all else fails, and we find ourselves in life's darkest moments, David reminds us that we do not have to be consumed by fear—God will be with us.

His Rod Equals Power

Earlier I noted that the shepherd's rod was a powerful weapon used to protect sheep. If you were a shepherd, you learned who the enemy was. You knew the silhouettes of wolves and the sounds of lions on the prowl. You were fully trained in the use of the rod to kill any predator. When you were taking your flock through dark and uncertain places, you'd stand ready to protect them. It made sense that the sheep would draw comfort from such powerful protections. Likewise, at times in your life when you are in dangerous territory, remind

62

yourself that your Shepherd is with you, he has a rod—and he knows how to use it!

You and I, as God's sheep, have a deadly predator that 1 Peter 5:8 warns us about, "Be self-controlled and alert. Your enemy the devil prowls around like a roaring lion looking for someone to devour." This is a real danger, and when we are going through tough times, we may be more inclined to stray, which makes us even more vulnerable to the enemy of our souls. We need to remain alert and let our Shepherd lead us on the "paths of righteousness." Most importantly, we need to stay close to our Shepherd because he has the power to fend off the enemy's attacks against us. But you might ask, "How does that work? How can I stay close to the shepherd when in my fear and insecurities I'm prone to stray away?" The answer is in God's staff.

His Staff Equals God's Word

The shepherd's staff corresponds to the way God's Word functions in our lives. When a sheep strays, the shepherd taps the sheep with his staff to get him back on the safe path, thus correcting him. The shepherd uses the crook of the staff to lift a sheep out of a ditch. As the shepherd walks along, the sheep can see the staff standing tall beside him and follow it. The Bible says, "All Scripture is God-breathed and is useful for teaching, rebuking, correcting and training in righteousness, so that the man of God may be thoroughly equipped for every good work" (2 Tim. 3:16–17). So God's Word serves the same functions as the shepherd's staff.

Following God's Word is crucial to making it through the dark valleys. I don't know about you, but when things get dark or I have to go through something that I'd rather avoid, the enemy starts to throw lies at me, giving me ideas about shortcuts like these:

✓ "Hey, does your marriage seem a little stale? Turn it in and try another one."

✓ "Feel bored? Depressed? Down? Go shopping!"

✓ "You're tired of so and so? Ignore them."

✓ "You got financial needs? Just charge it!"
✓ "Take life in your own hands—make yourself happy for a change."

But those suggestions take us far from the paths of righteousness. When the valley is dark, you need to make sure you stay on the right path. When the enemy comes in and tempts you to go your own way, don't fall for it! Follow the staff of your shepherd; follow God's Word. I can't tell you how many times the simple, habitual practice of getting into God's Word every morning (regardless of how I feel) has restored my soul and kept me from disaster.

Prepare for a Banquet

God took David through the dark valleys, staying with him all the way, providing, protecting, and keeping all his promises. But life is more than difficulties and darkness. On the other side of the valley, a banquet is waiting. David's psalm ends with a tribute to the some of the highlights of a godly life. Look at Psalm 23:5–6:

> You prepare a table before me
>   in the presence of my enemies.
> You anoint my head with oil;
>   my cup overflows.
> Surely goodness and love will follow me
>   all the days of my life,
> and I will dwell in the house of the LORD
>   forever.

In these closing verses, the psalmist does something interesting. He takes the sheep and shepherd metaphor and gently lays it on the shelf. Then he comes over and reaches for another metaphor common to his culture. He's not going to end this psalm on a negative note. He's going to celebrate the fullness of God's character and what he has in store for those who follow him even in the midst of crisis. So the metaphor changes to a banquet. In sharp contrast to the darkness of the valley and the dangers of the journey, David writes of a feast, a celebration filled with food, music, joy, and happy relationships. God serves as the gracious host.

A Table Is Prepared

As the door of the banquet hall swings open, David sees a wonderful sight. He says in wonder, "You prepare a table before me in the presence of my enemies." This is a great picture. In the ancient Near Eastern culture, eating a meal meant far more than going to a fast-food restaurant. It was a fellowship, especially a banquet. To "prepare a table" gives the idea of a big celebration. After a great military victory, the general who won would ride in literally on a white horse (such imagery can also be found in Psalm 68 and Ephesians 4). He would enter the gates with his troops, bringing in the plunder and then all the captives. While the defeated foe watched, the people would hold a great celebration, giving credit to their gods for the great victory. This would lead to a grand feast. Such banquets were held to publicly declare that the victor's god was greater than the gods of the vanquished.

This idea of fellowship at a banquet table, and the closeness of such fellowship, can be seen many places in Scripture, especially in passages that foretell our final victory feast in heaven. David may have started this psalm with the truth that we are like sheep, following our shepherd through difficult and dangerous transitions, but he ended it with thoughts of eternity. The way we find the courage to keep following God is to look forward to the victory he assures us is ours in the future. God is calling us to enter in. He's assuring us that even though we go through crises in this life, he is leading us on to certain victory over our enemies.

Our joy comes from fellowship with him. "Sit down and eat with me," God calls. Revelation 3:20 says, "Here I am! I stand at the door and knock; if anyone [any person, any woman, any child, any student] hears my voice and opens the door, I will come in and eat with him, and he with me." Don't miss that last promise. To those who welcome him, God says, "I will come in and eat with him, and he with me." Eating in the Bible is always a picture of fellowship, unity, communion, and relationship with God. And the by-product is joy.

Abundant Joy, Overflowing

Notice the phrase "you anoint my head with oil, my cup overflows." In biblical days, if you were the host of a huge victory banquet, you anointed the guests as they arrived. The host would take olive oil, mix it with perfume and spices, and pour it on the guests as an honor. This was also an official welcome to a celebration. The act announced, "You are special!"

Once the guests were seated, the servants kept the cups overflowing to underscore the welcome and joy. God is not giving out goodness in eyedroppers. The overflowing cup is a symbol of abundance and joy! It's not like, "Watch how much you eat. No second helpings!" Instead, these details convey the idea that, "There's the table. It is filled. It is all for you. It is lavish, and there's plenty more where that came from." It's a picture of God's goodness. He wants to do good things for us—spiritually and in every other way.

Look at What's Following You

"Surely goodness and love will follow me." The word "follow" here actually means "pursue." That's right, God is actually pursuing you with his love and goodness. But if you unconsciously look at life through the grid of CNN's, Fox Network's, ABC's, and CBS's nightly news, you could get the impression that the world is a bad, bad, bad place. If you listen to them too much, you might begin looking over your shoulder to make sure nothing evil sneaks up on you. While it is true that we live in a fallen world, David assures us that our lives are watched over by a good God who makes sure that goodness and love (mercy) will follow us all the days of our lives. The word "goodness" literally means "lavish love." "Mercy" is a word that refers to God's steadfast, loyal, and covenant commitment to you that never stops. God's mercy doesn't just lag along behind you, it's pursuing you. How long? All the days of your life.

Look What Your Future Holds

Psalm 23 ends with this assurance, "I will dwell in the house of the LORD forever." That is David's third and final confident affirmation. He sees God as his Shepherd, who promises an abundant life now and forever. "Abundant life," doesn't that ring a bell? Remember what Jesus said in John 10:10? "I came that they may have life, and have it abundantly" (NASB). The word literally means "spilling over, overflowing." It doesn't necessarily mean that you're going to drive fancy cars, have a great house, and never have a problem. It means you're going to overflow from the inside out, having more than enough to get you through whatever you have to go through because God is with you and will take you all the way through all life's transitions, until you arrive in his house and rejoice there forever! It can be rich, it can be deep, it can be powerful, it can be wonderful, and it can be that regardless of what dark valleys you have to go through along the way. That's what it means to have an abundant life—here and hereafter. And to punctuate his purpose, immediately after promising us abundant life, Jesus reveals his identity. "I am the good shepherd" (John 10:11 NASB).

Experiencing God as Your Good Shepherd

God has promised not only that his goodness and mercy will follow us all the days of our lives but also that we will feast at his banqueting table. Since before eternity, God will demonstrate his abundance in surprising ways to those who trust him. We can experience his presence as our Good Shepherd every day. In upcoming chapters I tell the stories of many people who have experienced God's character in special ways, but to close this chapter I'd like to share with you the story I know best—my own.

The Rest of the Story

My journey was a difficult one as I struggled to follow God and make the right decision about getting married. I don't have room here to give you all the details of how he led Theresa and me together. That might be exciting for me, but a bit boring for you. What I can tell you is that in ways that were unmistakable and even supernatural, God showed us it was in fact his will and his best for us to marry. God brought us (me in particular) through the shadows of the valley of indecision. I experienced his patient shepherding in my life.

68

That was over twenty-three years ago. I'm now the proud father of those young twin boys. In the providence of God, I had the opportunity to adopt them. Our relationship is beyond my wildest dreams in terms of intimacy and love for one another. The father-son connection didn't happen overnight. In fact, it took years for the bond to grow. Eric is now a physical therapist and lives near us in Santa Cruz, California. I marvel as I watch God use him to bring life and healing to others. Jason is a Christian recording artist who lives in Nashville and is in full-time ministry, using the talents given him by God. They are not only my sons but two of my closest friends. I can't imagine life without them.

As a special bonus, God granted us two other children. Our third son, Ryan, is presently at Moody Bible Institute studying for the ministry. He, like his older brother, takes after his mom. He is musically gifted and loves to lead worship, play drums, and share Christ. Our youngest is a girl who came along a little bit later in our life. Annie is now a vibrant teen. She grew up in a home with three older brothers, who are all quite protective and have helped her become a young, beautiful, godly woman. She has a heart to serve others, is gifted musically, and is mature beyond her years.

This may sound a little bit like a fairy tale, but it's not. I'm sharing the wonderful results. The process has been hard. Many decisions along the way were tough, and the original crisis was real. But God does promise a banqueting table, and my family has turned out better than my wildest dreams. We don't have it all together and every day is not a big party; but our relationships are rich and deep. Our love for each other is solid. God has granted me the deepest desires of my heart. The Good Shepherd took me through the shadow of the valley of death, and his goodness and his mercy have pursued me ever since.

I know some reading these words are in the midst of intense pain and crisis. You long for the dark valley to end and the banquet table to appear. You want to honor God, but it's difficult and you may not know how. I'd like to close this chapter by giving you five practical life lessons from this psalm to help you experience God as your shepherd in your time of crisis.

LIFE LESSON 1: Make the Lord Your Shepherd

Let me repeat that because it is so crucial. Make the Lord your shepherd! Put differently, allow Christ to be Lord of your life. Stop right now and submit your will, your agenda, your future, and your fears to him. If you do, then all these promises in Psalm 23 apply to you.

The other option is to say, "You know something? I'm a pretty big sheep. I'll go graze where I think I'll be fulfilled. I'll follow the other sheep and go where I think it'll be fun." What happens when a real sheep does that? It soon has big problems. The same holds true for people. You see, the biggest problem in our lives is not that God is mean or that he doesn't really care about us; the biggest problem comes from the fact that down deep in our hearts we are proud and self-sufficient. Most people want to be both the sheep and the shepherd. I know that's how I was before I began following Jesus, and I continue to struggle with that to some degree every day. So the first step is to admit that you are a sheep in need of a shepherd, and then ask the Lord to be *your* shepherd. He wants to help you!

LIFE LESSON 2: Determine to Follow the Lord as Your Shepherd

Knowing what is right to do and doing it are two different things. God cares about you far more than you can imagine. He knows the dangers, the pain, the hurt, and the fear that you feel. He wants what's best for you and wants to lead you and direct you even more than you want to be led. Choose to do what you know is right according to Scripture even when every fiber in your being wants to bail out. If you will follow, he will lead you in paths of righteousness. You will, in the midst of your crisis, endure short-term pain. But if you will follow by faith, you will experience long-term gain. Trust him!

LIFE LESSON 3: Refuse to Let Fear Dominate Your Life

Do this especially during times of transition, when things are uncertain and you have to make decisions that have momentous consequences. We learn this from David's declaration, "I will fear no evil." Fearless living is a choice. God is willing to see us through, but we have to be strong and courageous to continue following him through those valleys. Courage is not the absence of fear. Courage is trusting God and his Word even when circumstances seem impossible. Memorize Isaiah 40:31, and say it often when you feel fear's grip upon your soul.

LIFE LESSON 4: Be on Guard against the Enemy

Be on guard against the enemy of your soul, the devil, and resist him. It takes strength and courage to resist the predatory attacks of Satan. I looked up the word "strong" in several dictionaries. Strength is described as a quality of having force, power, or vigor; the power to resist strain and stress. Strength incorporates toughness and durability. It is the power to resist attack. Strength refers to the inherent capacity to act upon or affect something to endure or to resist.

How do you measure strength? One accurate way is to measure strength by how much you can resist. We say that someone who can lift a hundred pounds over their head is strong. If you can lift two hundred pounds over your head, you are stronger, right? What are weights? They represent levels of gravity that you can overcome. When we say you are strong, we really mean you can overcome a huge amount of resistance. In spiritual terms we need to resist the devil (James 4:7), resist the temptation to take short-cuts, and exercise strength to overcome every obstacle along the way as we follow our shepherd.

71

LIFE LESSON 5: Get in the Scripture Daily

God told another ancient wise sheep, Joshua, "Only be strong and very courageous; be careful to do according to all the law which Moses my servant commanded you; do not turn from it to the right or to the left" (Josh. 1:7 NASB). Why? So that you may have success wherever you go. The word "careful" literally means "to observe"; it means to look into for the purposes of putting into practice. God was telling Joshua, "I want you to follow my instructions down to the detail, doing everything that I commanded Moses." God showed David the same truth. The more we know of God's Word and the more we make it a part of us, the more its power to comfort, convict, direct, and empower us.

Why Follow the Lord as Your Shepherd?

Why does God want us to let him be our shepherd and follow the life lessons above? For the same reasons David understood when he said, "Surely goodness and love will follow me all the days of my life and I will dwell in the house of the LORD forever." When the Lord is our shepherd, good results will follow. God gave Joshua the same reason, "so that you can be successful." The word "successful" literally means, "to be prudent." It has the idea of seeking after God and following him in such a way that you will actually live your life according to his plan. Success here didn't guarantee that Joshua would get a new chariot or you a new BMW. The success you'll have if you will follow the Lord and his Word, not turning to the right or the left, is that you can be guided in the same way that Moses, Joshua, and David were guided by God.

The success promised here is that you will be able to discern what to do in every situation, trusting that God can lead you and make your way prosperous. The Hebrew word here for "prosperous" literally means "you will make your way with power and ability to fulfill the will of God." Be strong and courageous; don't tremble; don't be dismayed. Why? For the Lord your God is with you wherever you go. Keep following the Lord as your shepherd. Trust in his provision, his presence, and his power to protect you. Keep following his Word. Then he will fulfill his promise to take you to the green pastures and still waters you long for. He will lead you on to celebrate victory in this life and in the one to come.

LIFE LESSONS TO APPLY

1. Make the Lord your shepherd.

2. Follow the Lord with all your heart.

3. Refuse to let fear dominate your life.

4. Be on guard against the enemy.

5. Get in the Scripture daily.

EXPERIENCING GOD THROUGH TIMES OF CRISIS

Somewhere you can turn: Psalm 23

KEY VERSES

The LORD is my shepherd, I shall not be in want.
Even though I walk
through the valley of the shadow of death,
I will fear no evil,
for you are with me;
your rod and your staff,
they comfort me.

Psalm 23:1, 4

3

I am with you . . .

WHEN YOU
FEEL LIKE A
NOBODY
GOING
NOWHERE

If you've never seen the movie *Mr. Holland's Opus*, I recommend it highly. It provides one of the rare occasions when Hollywood actually captured a timeless truth God wants us to understand. In case you haven't seen the movie, here's a quick review. A man spends thirty years raising a family and teaching high school music. He not only teaches his subjects, he pours his life and his gifts into his students. As the story unfolds, we discover that he took the teaching job because he couldn't make a living writing and performing his own music. Throughout his thirty-year career his life dream of composing a symphony has simmered on a back burner. Finally, his music program is axed because of financial cutbacks. It feels like he has given his whole life and for what?

One of the scenes near the end of the movie captures the outlook of a man who feels like a nobody going nowhere. What bright future can he see? Maybe he can teach a few piano lessons. What of his dream of changing lives, impacting students, and giving the gift of music to the next generation? Those dreams have come crashing to a halt. How were his long hours and dedication rewarded? By little recognition, low pay, and finally the termination of his music program.

In this scene, Bill, the football coach and a friend for thirty years, comes into the music room where Mr. Holland is seated on his piano bench. They exchange a painful dialogue:

Bill: I wanted to see if you needed any help.
Mr. Holland: Nope. Nope, nope, nope.
Bill: So, you decided what you're going to do yet?

Mr. Holland: Too old to start a rock band, . . . probably hang out a shingle and teach a few piano lessons.

Bill: I'd love to retire . . .

Mr. Holland: I'm not retiring, Bill. I'm getting dumped. And I don't think you have anything to worry about. The day they cut the football budget in this state, well now, that will be the end of Western civilization as we know it. (He pauses and grows somber) . . . I'll tell you the truth. I'm scared to death . . .

Bill: They have no idea how much they're going to miss you around here.

Mr. Holland: You really think so?

Bill: What? And you doubt it?

Mr. Holland: Well, as a matter of fact, yeah. It's almost funny. I got dragged into this gig kicking and screaming and now it's the only thing I want to do and . . . You work your whole life . . . You work for thirty years because you think that what you do makes a difference; you think it matters to people. Then you wake up one morning, and you find out; well no, you've made a little error there. You are expendable. Oh, God, I should be laughing . . .

His voice trails off. His friend pats him on the back before leaving, and Mr. Holland is left sitting alone on his piano bench in an empty classroom.

Do You Ever Feel like a Nobody Going Nowhere?

Do you ever feel that way? I mean, down deep. When it's quiet and everybody else is in bed, or when you're driving and you don't have to pay too much attention, do you start thinking about where your life is headed, what you've done or haven't done? Do you start adding up what your life amounts to and you come up short? At those times, do you feel like a nobody going nowhere? Has the thought ever crossed your mind, "If I was gone, a week later, no one would notice. Maybe a few family members, but no one would really notice." Ever feel that way? Do you ever feel like you're on a treadmill? There's a lot of activity, but you're not getting anywhere; you're working hard, but it doesn't amount to much? If so, you're not alone. Lots of people feel like that; but their perception is not necessarily true.

Most people who take time to reflect on their lives struggle with these kinds of thoughts and feelings at some point. Some people wrestle with such feelings every day, others only occasionally. This is not something I struggle with on a day-to-day basis, but I've had real struggles in this area at critical times in my life. One two-year period between 1988 and 1990, toward the end of my time in Texas, taught me a lot about the feeling of going nowhere.

Is Your Life Different Than You Expected?

During seminary I accepted a pastorate at a little church thirty-two miles outside of Dallas, Texas. The town was home to forty-five hundred people but lacked enough traffic to need a single stoplight. We started out with about thirty-five people in the church. I made a five-year commitment. I finished my schooling in the first two years and stayed on the next three. We were deeply loved. They were great people. The church grew. In many ways it was a wonderful situation. But as I completed my five-year commitment and stayed on into the sixth year, I started comparing my life to my early hopes and dreams. I was staring at a big gap between what I had expected and the life I was living.

You see, I went to school to be a missionary. I wanted God to use my life to reach the world. That was my motivation. Before being called into ministry, I'd been a coach and a teacher. When God called, I said, "Okay, Lord, I'll do this," but I did it with high hopes and lofty aspirations. I had already gone to college, then on to graduate school, then on to seminary. It was a long journey and a lot of hard work. But all that effort was okay because I was going somewhere. Then I stopped to look at my life after six years in that first church, and I thought to myself, "Wait, I never signed up to be a pastor. I wanted to be a missionary. Besides, if I was going to be a pastor, I certainly would not have chosen a small town in Texas."

What Happened to Your Dreams?

So after all those years of education and six years of serving faithfully in that church, I found myself feeling like a nobody. I took stock of my life. I reflected on all the dreams, visions, and hopes I started out with. I went back over how I had come to this point in my life. That didn't help quell those feelings that I was going nowhere. Most days I traveled in a radius of about two miles around our church. As I made that little circuit, I counted sixteen churches. Sixteen! I kept thinking, "If someone wants to hear the gospel in Kaufman, Texas, they can hear it from any of these churches. They certainly don't need me here! Is this why I went through all the struggle to be in a town of forty-five hundred people without a stoplight? God, is this where I'm going to land? What about those promises from Scripture? What about those dreams I started out with? What about having a great impact on the world? Hey, God, what about really using me? This is it?" There was about a two-year stretch when I thought God had forgotten my name. I felt like my dreams were dying and I was a nobody going nowhere.

When Do You Feel like a Nobody Going Nowhere?

How about you? Do you struggle with such feelings? Maybe it's related to a job. Maybe you've been at it a long time and don't feel appreciated; maybe the younger generation seems to be getting all the breaks while you're overlooked. Maybe you're just starting out, but your boss or coworkers don't take you seriously. You don't feel significant or needed or recognized for what you contribute. Maybe you feel like a nobody because you think you don't become a *somebody* until you get married, or until you have a child, or until you accomplish something great. Maybe your spouse, or boss, or some other significant person doesn't appreciate you. The list goes on, but for a variety of reasons you may be coming to the same kind of conclusions as Mr. Holland. You may be retired, looking back in the rearview mirror or at midlife and thinking, "If I don't get with it, this is all I'm going to have for the rest of my life." Or perhaps you're young and saying, "What does it matter anyway? No one gives a rip." Whoever you are, at whatever stage of life, I'm here to tell you that you do matter. Someone does care. You are a somebody destined to go somewhere—because God says so.

Do you want to know how it works? Keep reading!

Warning: Perceptions Are Not Reality

How you perceive your life, your value, your destiny doesn't give you the whole picture. You may be seeing yourself and your significance dimly. But your self-perception determines in large measure the way your life will go. What you believe about yourself—whether it's true or not—will influence your relationship with God, your attitude, endeavors, and how you face life's challenges. The issue of your significance and purpose is important. Therefore, it is vital that those deep questions at the core of your being are answered with truth. Dim or mistaken perceptions that aren't in keeping with reality must be challenged and corrected by the light of God's Word.

Remember the story in the introduction, of our friend Michael who came barreling to our door because he believed his life was in danger from a ferocious dog? His perception determined his response. When the porch light went on, he saw reality. Only then did his response become appropriate. Likewise, our self-perception, estimation of our worth and purpose, can be misread when viewed in the dim light of daily existence. We need the light of God's revealed truth to see the whole picture, so we can respond appropriately. Our need is for more than just knowledge. We need the hope that God's truth can stir in us. God provides the kind of light we need in Psalm 139.

PSALM 139

If you believe you're a nobody going nowhere, you're not seeing the whole picture. Your view needs to be corrected in the light of God's truth. In Psalm 139 God gives us five truths that can help us see ourselves as he sees us. So sit back, relax, put your feet up, and turn to Psalm 139. And if you're feeling like a nobody going nowhere, tell the Lord, "That's how I feel right now, Lord. Please show me it's not true."

LIFE LESSON 1: God Knows You

Look at Psalm 139:1–6 and note the words I have italicized:

> O LORD, you have *searched* me
>   and you *know* me.
> You *know* when I sit and when I rise;
>   you *perceive* my thoughts from afar.
> You *discern* my going out and my lying down;
>   you are *familiar* with all my ways.
> Before a word is on my tongue
>   you *know* it completely, O LORD.

> You *hem* me in—behind and before;
> you have *laid* your hand upon me.
> Such knowledge is too wonderful for me,
> too lofty for me to attain.

I have italicized nine references with different Hebrew words that tell you in different ways that God knows you intimately. He knows your heart, your fears, thoughts, motives, dreams, and frustrations. He knows your past, present, and your future—and he's involved in it. God knows you. God understands you. When you are frustrated, when you're afraid, when you feel like a nobody, when you wonder what's up—whatever you are going through or whatever is going through your mind, God knows. You are on God's mind. He is noticing what's going on with you, to you, and around you. Even though you may not be able to see what he's doing at the moment, he is working. He is operating in your life in ways that you may not be able to see clearly. Before you get up, he knows where you are. He knows when you sit down. When a thought comes to your mind, God knows all about it before it gets formulated in your cranium. Think of it—God already knows you tomorrow!

In fact, God understands you infinitely more than you understand yourself. You think you do certain things for this reason or that; you think your motives are *A* when God knows they are really *B*. You think you've got a feel for how you come off with people; you think you understand the kind of mom or dad you really are. You know what? You really don't. You and I see ourselves as shadows through a dim, dark glass, but he sees us clearly. He knows you.

That can be a pretty scary thought, but not to worry. Not only does God know you, he gives reassurance that his knowledge is integrated with great love. When David says that God laid his hand upon him, he's referring to an Old Testament phrase that means the intimate act of blessing. Before an old man died, he would lay his hands on the heads of his children and grandchildren to speak hopeful words into their lives. This ancient act had all the dignity and legal standing of a final will. The blessing was (and is) a powerful gift.

God's hand is laid upon you for your blessing and protection. His knowledge of you is couched in his love and concern, just as good parents know their children and look out for their well-being in keeping with that knowledge.

LIFE LESSON 2: God Is Pursuing You

The second thing you need to remember is that God is pursuing you. Notice how the psalmist responded to his own awareness of God's intimacy? He said, "It's too wonderful, it's too lofty." The words there mean that "it's incomprehensible, it's overwhelming." David got a glimpse into who God is, and he just can't take it. His first response is as if to say, "I just can't deal with it." His second response, however, is probably what most of ours would be. If God knows everything—and everything means everything—what would most of us want to do? We'd want to run. We would feel suddenly unmasked. We would remember all those times we do something nice and try to look very Christian, very kind; but we know we have ulterior motives. Our real goal involves wanting people to think better of us, so we project things that aren't true.

Is God intimately aware of all of that? Yes. You mean the gig is up? Yes. Well if that's the case, it's not only too lofty, it may be too painful. You mean God sees all the warts? Uh-hum. He knows all the secrets? Every one. Well, we have a problem then, don't we? It's interesting. Often when people feel like nobodies, they want to run away from God and people. David certainly thought about escape.

God Isn't Going to Let You Run Away

> Where can I go from your Spirit?
> Where can I flee from your presence?
> If I go up to the heavens, you are there;
> if I make my bed in the depths, you are there.

> If I rise on the wings of the dawn,
> if I settle on the far side of the sea,
> even there your hand will guide me,
> your right hand will hold me fast.
>
> verses 7–10

Verses 7 through 10 teach us that God isn't going to let us run away. God is pursuing you. When the psalmist asked, "Where can I go from your Spirit?" and, "Where can I flee from your presence?" he was asking rhetorical questions. He already knew the answer—nowhere. God, I can't escape you!

The psalmist reviewed his potential spiritual and geographical escape routes. He started with the heights, then the depths; looked east, then west—then concluded, "Even there your hand will guide me and your right hand will hold me fast." He realized that we can't get away from God—not geographically and not spiritually.

God Is in a Different Category Altogether

> If I say, "Surely the darkness will hide me
> and the light become night around me,"
> even the darkness will not be dark to you;
> the night will shine like the day,
> for darkness is as light to you.
>
> verses 11–12

If we delude ourselves by thinking, "Surely the darkness will hide me," the psalmist stops us with the realization that "even the darkness will not be dark" to God. He says to God, "The night will shine like the day, for darkness is as light to you." What a great line!

David is showing us how different God is from us. This truth has almost been lost in our generation. God is holy. That means he is other. God isn't just bigger and better, he is in a different category altogether. We tend to think of God as an enlarged, super human being. We have intelligence, so we think that God must

85

have five "X" more intelligence. We think of a loving person, then we think God must be a million times more loving. That's not correct. God is not just the best of humanity magnified, he is totally different, totally other. There isn't a category for him. He's one of a kind. For us, there's either light or darkness; but light and darkness are all the same to God. God is light; the light and darkness of our reality are simply part of a complex system that he authored. He's above them; he's beyond them.

Even though we can never flee God, his desire in pursuing us is not to bring about condemnation but to bring about forgiveness, and friendship, and love. Notice where it says, "Your hand will guide me"—that's direction. "Your right hand will hold me fast"— that's security. Wherever you are, however lonely, however you might try to run from God, from truth, from life, from important people, God is pursuing you to bring about your well-being.

You Are Desirable to God!

Are you ready for this? You are wanted by God. He's pursuing you. You are valuable. You are desirable! He's pursuing you, but not to point out all that's wrong with you. He's pursuing you because he desires an intimate relationship with you.

This idea is staggering. We see its impact in the Bible story of the Samaritan woman who met Jesus at a well. She was surprised, first of all, that a Jewish man would even speak to her. The Jews of the time had no dealings with the Samaritans because of intense racial hatred and religious conflict. Not only did Jesus talk to her, he shocked her by revealing that he knew all the intimate—and shameful—details of her life. He knew everything she had ever done, including her five marriages and the fact that she was currently living with a man who was not her husband.

However, he didn't use his knowledge to condemn her. Instead he stunned her with the revelation that God wasn't particularly interested in the religious questions she brought up. What God was really after, what God was pursuing, was her. Jesus revealed the heavenly Father as one who is actively pursuing and seeking worshipers who will worship him in spirit and in truth. The Gospel of Luke backs this up when Jesus explains his reason for coming to the earth. He said, "I came to seek and to save that which was lost." *God is pursuing you every moment of every day.*

The Bible is filled with references that show that God values us so much more than we think he does, especially when we're feeling like a nobody. God calls his people "the apple of his eye"; believers are called the object of his affection. In the New Testament, God calls those who are his beloved, chosen, holy, dearly loved; we are told that nothing and no one can ever separate us from the love of God in Christ. Nothing. When you feel like a nobody you need to remind yourself that God understands how you feel because he knows you completely. You need to remember that you are wanted in a very special way.

Remember the First Time Someone Wanted You?

Do you remember the first time a girl or a guy was interested in you? It may have been in junior high, high school, or college. Do you remember what it felt like when you knew you were wanted in a special way? I watched it happen all the time when I was a teacher. The way it works in junior high is like this: Mary tells Joe who tells Bob who tells Karen that her friend Anita is interested in you. Karen tells you. Then you walk around the lunchroom, sneaking peeks in Anita's direction. Suddenly your eyes meet briefly and quickly look away. Then you notice she's smiling. Remember how that felt? Remember how good it felt? You know why? You were wanted.

Oh, the games we play! Do you remember standing in a crowd on the playing field and hearing someone say, "I want you on my team," and they pointed at you? Do you remember that? Not that different from having a corporation recruit you, is it? Do you know how it feels to have an interviewer stop the interview before it was even over and say, "I would really like you to work for us"? Have you ever had someone say, "I want you to be my friend"? There's something very powerful about these moments, isn't there? You know why? Because something inside our heart says, "Me? Really?"

Can you stop for a moment and attempt to grasp that someone beyond the best looking or the greatest man or woman on the earth, beyond the best employer or the best team, wants you. Right now you may feel like a nobody, but the God of the universe says, "I want you! I love you! I want to be your friend. I would like you on my team. Yes, I am pursuing you."

One writer captured this idea by describing God as "the hound of heaven." He will not relent in pursuit of your heart, your soul, and your affection until it is his or it is too late. That's how God feels about every unbeliever; that's how God feels about every believer. He doggedly pursues us and gives us all the opportunity to either accept his pursuing and persistent love or to reject his advances.

LIFE LESSON 3: God Says You're Awesome

Are you beginning to see how important it is to get an accurate biblical perception of yourself? You're not a nobody in God's eyes! He knows you and wants you. And that's not all. It actually gets better! The third truth we need to remember when we feel like a nobody is that God made us.

> For you created my inmost being;
>> you knit me together in my mother's womb.
> I praise you because I am fearfully and wonderfully made;
>> your works are wonderful,
>> I know that full well.
> My frame was not hidden from you
>> when I was made in the secret place.
> When I was woven together in the depths of the earth,
>> your eyes saw my unformed body.
>
> verses 13–16a

Notice verse 13; those are strong descriptive words. In today's vernacular, the closest equivalent to the phrase "fearfully and wonderfully made" would be something like "You're totally awesome!" David goes on to say, "Your works are wonderful," speaking of the entire universe. But what is the pinnacle of all God's creation? It's not what, it's who—people—me and, yes, you. Each human being made in the image of God with the ability to think, love, choose, plan, dream, and care is the pinnacle of God's creation. The infinitely personal God is not a large version of us; rather, we are the image—the created beings who most share characteristics with our Creator.

He goes on to say, "My frame"—or my skeleton—"was not hidden from you when I was made in the secret place. When I was woven together in the depths of the earth your eyes saw my unformed substance." Look carefully at the words in those verses that relate to creation: "created," "knit," "made," "woven together," "unformed substance." The fact that you are made as you are gives evidence of how awesome you are to God. He was personally involved in your creation. I'll never forget when I first began to appreciate the wonder of how God made me.

How Are You Made?

I was taking a class at West Virginia University. At that point in my life, I thought that the greatest job in the world would be coaching a major NCAA Division I college with a great basketball tradition. In pursuit of that dream, I went back to graduate school. I took a course in advanced physiology. I can't remember the professor's name, but she made a lasting impact on me. She talked about the human body with reverence and awe. As far as I know, she was not a believer. But when she described the human anatomy and how it worked, down to all the intricate workings of the skeletal system, the brain, the neurons, and how all the systems of the human body interact to work together, she spoke with reverential passion. She would lecture in hushed tones, as if she were doing homage to the most beautiful thing that has ever been created. Her fascination was contagious. When she talked about the mechanics of the arm, elbow, wrist, and fingers, she raised her own hand to the light, as if the rest of us might be able to see through her skin the marvels that we took for granted every day.

I remember during one lecture when she picked up a bone that had been shattered. She said, "Do you see this bone? It has a compound fracture. Do you know what your body can do? Long before we learned to reset broken bones, the human body already knew what to do. It just took longer. Even with the complications of a fracture as bad as this, the human body will seek to repair the break precisely where it is needed. Over time, it will even attempt to straighten itself out."

She talked about the healing properties of the body and the miracle of the autonomic nervous system with a tone and attitude I was used to hearing only in church. I walked away thinking, "That lady understands more about holiness than the average church does." She displayed in the classroom what David expressed in this psalm.

David seems to say, "I'm created, but it's not just the physical part; there are awesome workings within my inmost being that are too great for us to fully comprehend." He wasn't talking as if God made us with no more thought than if he made a lump of clay. God didn't just create wandering neurons and protons that accidentally combined to result in you. You have God's handiwork written all over you. You're intricately made with a cardiovascular system, a nervous system, and all the other physical systems that work together to make up your body. That alone is awesome enough, but there's so much more. He made your psyche, your unique personality, and your DNA. He made you like no one else in the universe, in all of history. God knows that you are unique: in your thoughts, your feelings, your contribution, your gift mix, and your personality. He made you inside and out, body, mind, and spirit. In your innermost being, he knows you. And he treasures you as a unique person at the pinnacle of his creation.

LIFE LESSON 4: God Has a Plan Just for You

All the days ordained for me
were written in your book
before one of them came to be.

> How precious to me are your thoughts, O God!
> How vast is the sum of them!
> Were I to count them,
> they would outnumber the grains of sand.
> When I awake,
> I am still with you.
>
> verses 16b–18

When you read, "All the days ordained for me were written in [God's] book before one of them came to be," think, "God knows my calendar and God knows me." The word "ordained" is the same word as that used in Genesis when it says God fashioned or formed man out of the earth. It's not just that he knows our days in terms of how many, but it's the idea of being uniquely fashioned. We have a divine design that reminds us we're tailor-made by God for his glory and our good. Even though we have choices, God knows when life ends; he knew when it began. He is eternal. He sees the end from the beginning, and he uniquely gifted you and me for our special contribution.

Verses 17 and 18 describe how God thinks about people. Each of us fits into the divine scheme of things. God—who orchestrates the entire universe—is simultaneously thinking about the lives of individuals. Every day God thinks about you many times a day. He thinks about what you think and cares about what you feel. He is concerned about the things that concern you. Any moment you choose to turn your thoughts toward him, he is already thinking about you. You're on God's mind sixty minutes of every hour, twenty-four hours a day, seven days a week.

God Thinks about You Constantly

God thinks of you throughout the day because he cares about what is going on in your life. It's like this. Not long ago Theresa and I were traveling away from home while at the same time our daughter was on a snow trip with the youth group. At one point, Theresa looked at the clock and murmured, "Hmm . . . 3:59, the slopes close at 4:00, don't they?"

I said, "Yeah, I think so."

Then it dawned on me that her thoughts were continually tracking with our daughter. Out of sight—maybe; out of mind—never! Annie was getting up, she was having breakfast, she was out there snowboarding, and then she was going to bed. Even though Theresa was focused on what we were doing, her thoughts were keeping track of Annie, moment by moment. When you love someone, you think about what they are doing even when you are apart. We're never out of God's sight, nor are we ever out of his thoughts. It's just that he can manage infinitely more than we can conceive.

Do you know what God's doing right now? Among other things, he's thinking about you. He's thinking about your decisions. He's fully aware of the fears on your mind. The concerns you're carrying are on his heart. God doesn't miss the struggles you're facing or the temptations that are coming at you.

God Has a Plan

Psalm 139 says that God does have a plan for you. You can choose to cooperate with that plan, or you can choose to ignore it. God told Jeremiah to give a whole group of people, who were definitely feeling like nobodies going nowhere, this message, "'For I know the plans I have for you,' declares the LORD, 'plans to prosper you and not to harm you, plans to give you hope and a future'" (Jer. 29:11). Ephesians 2:10 says, "For we are God's workmanship, created in Christ Jesus to do good works, which God prepared in advance for us to do." See, God knows it all in advance! I believe this means that there are certain parts of what God wants to accomplish in the world that you were designed to bring about, something only you can do.

You Are a Vital Part of God's Plan

Here's where we tend to get hung up. Maybe your life is not what you think it ought to be, but God has choreographed all creation, and he created a special role just for you. He invites you to do your part. I think of it like this: Have you ever been in the middle of one of those repair projects when you suddenly realize there are lots more little parts than you anticipated? I am not very good at that kind of thing, so it usually takes me two hours to put something together that would take a normal person half an hour. The added time isn't my biggest problem. My ultimate challenge comes when I'm just about finished with the ordeal, and I find that I need one more screw to finish. I have other screws, but they are bigger, or longer, or shorter, or they don't have the right threads. All I need is one screw—one specific screw—and the whole thing would work. Without that one little screw, the project is little more than a complicated doorstop. Now you tell me how important is that one screw? That's what I think God says about each human being he created. We were made to fill a place no one else can fill. God created the whole kit in advance and intended for each person to fulfill a specific place and role in life.

How Important Are You?

You were made to fulfill a purpose no one else can quite fill. Now, let me ask you, *How important are you?* You don't have to be up front. You don't have to be known. You don't have to have extraordinary gifts. Do you know what you need to do? You need to find out what part you were designed to fill in the divine plan and be available to fulfill your role. You get to actively cooperate with God! That little missing screw didn't make up the whole project and neither do you. You are designed to work in a synergistic body of people devoted to God and his plan, so that all the parts accomplish things far beyond what any individual could do.

Whether you play a modest or a more visible part, God created you to fulfill a vital role. In fact, I will be so bold as to say that God created you to be indispensable to the fulfillment of his overall plan. Sure, many people don't cooperate with God's plan for their lives, and the world doesn't fall apart. Will God, who is all-powerful and all-knowing, accomplish his work if you reject his plan and don't fulfill your part? You bet! But will it be the ideal ultimate result that he desired? No. You are indispensable to God. "Do you not know that your body is a temple of the Holy Spirit, who is in you, whom you have received from God? You are not your own; you were bought at a price. Therefore honor God with your body" (1 Cor. 6:19–20).

God has general purposes. For example, it's God's desire that everyone would come to faith in him. It's his desire that every believer would mature. But God also has a plan just for you that has to do with using your gifts and doing what God has designed you to be able to do. Among his desires are that you would discover your spiritual gifts and use them, that you would understand where you fit in the body, that you would team up with other believers, and that you would have great joy and satisfaction in being a part of God's plan. God intends that you experience fulfillment as his plan is fulfilled in and through you.

Two Potential Obstacles

There are two potential obstacles that could keep God's plan from being fulfilled in your life: the level of your cooperation and the level of your commitment.

R.S.V.P.

The first potential obstacle is that you need to invite him to work his plan in your life. He's got a plan, but he doesn't impose it on you. He waits for your response. We see this aspect of God's disposition toward his people in his words to a particular church in the Book of Revelation. "Here I am! I stand at the door and knock. If anyone hears my voice and opens the door, I will come in and eat with him, and he with me" (Rev. 3:20).

God doesn't just barge in and force his plan on you. This is part of what sets humanity above all the rest of creation. God allows us a great deal of freedom in whether or not we will comply with his will. You can sign up for God's plan or you can follow your own plan. If you sign up for God's plan, you become a part of his intricate workmanship created in Christ Jesus (created to accomplish good works God prepared in advance). When you sign on and accept God's plans for your life, you enter into what he preordained before the foundations of the earth. Whatever the specifics of that plan, they include that God would get glory and that it would be for your good. If you insist on your own plan,

94

decide to do life your way instead of God's way, if you stiff-arm God when it comes to his will for you, you will miss his best. As a result, your deepest needs, the God-inspired aspirations at the depths of your heart, will go unattended. God made you for himself. Sure, you can keep him at bay; but if you do, you will end up putting people, or money, or success, or work before God. Those who choose to reject God's plan in favor of their own plan end up filling their hearts with stuff; but their lives are empty even if they seem to have everything! There is simply no substitute for the joy and fulfillment that comes when our hearts and lives are aligned with God's purposes.

Commitment

Participating in God's plan involves more than an initial response. Every day includes new opportunities to cooperate with his purposes. We must also follow when God leads us in unexpected directions. Some of us became believers and accepted God's plan when we invited Christ into our lives, but problems have developed because we hold to rigid, preconceived notions about what God's plan must be. If we do that, we are not open to the leading of God's Spirit. If we rigidly hold to our notions of what his purposes and plans for us must be, we invite disappointment. If we think we absolutely know what God's goals and dreams are, our expectations can become our idols. What we thought God was going to do displaces our willingness to follow God's leading. The Bible calls this mistake "walking by sight, not by faith." It is possible to be so insistent on what we once thought was God's plan for us that we can't hear what he's actually trying to tell us about the next phase of our lives. For me that meant letting go of my demand to be a missionary. I was so bent and focused on that one area of service, I almost missed God's calling upon my life to be a pastor.

How about you? Have your expectations kept you from hearing God's voice clearly?

Stop, Listen, Yield

To know and fulfill God's plan for your life, you must regularly stop, listen afresh to what God is trying to get through to you, and yield again to his leading in your life. God longs for you to know his plan even more than you want to know it. He also knows you couldn't understand the entire plan right now, so he allows you to see what you need to see for the next step. This becomes a day-to-day adventure. Whenever you start feeling like a nobody going nowhere, that's the time to stop and remind yourself of the life lessons from Psalm 139: God knows you; he's pursuing you; he made you and has a purpose for your life. If all of that is true—and it is—you can't be a nobody going nowhere. But it means you will have to slow down, take time to read his Word, and sit quietly to hear his voice. Isn't it time to look at your life and circumstances from his perspective?

I can bet that you're thinking something like this: Well, if all that's true—and I hope that it is—why is my life stuck where it is? If God is always thinking fondly of me, why do I feel so unloved? If God is pursuing me, why do I feel so alone? If God wants me to experience the fulfillment of my life's purpose, why can't I see it? Why aren't these life lessons working?

LIFE LESSON 5: God's World Is Darkened by Sin

> If only you would slay the wicked, O God!
>   Away from me, you bloodthirsty men!
> They speak of you with evil intent;
>   your adversaries misuse your name.
> Do I not hate those who hate you, O Lord,
>   and abhor those who rise up against you?
> I have nothing but hatred for them;
>   I count them my enemies.
>
> verses 19–22

The final section in Psalm 139 may seem out of place at first reading. After the personal reflections in the first eighteen verses, the next four verses present a very strong, abrupt shift. This change helps us remember two significant factors that affect our experiences as believers. One factor is that God's goodness to us and plans for us must be worked out in a world of continual opposition. God's creation and plans are good, but evil has been introduced into this world and into every human life, bringing with it the potential for everything to get messed up. If evil holds sway, whether that is in the physical creation, human relationships, or in a single human heart, the results will be disastrous. That is why, in these verses, we see such a violent opposition to evil in immediate contrast to the good God intends for people he loves.

The second factor behind the abrupt shift in tone is that God's light of truth has been flipped on for the psalmist. When the lights come on in our soul, it changes everything. It changes not only how we see ourselves and how we see God but also how we see the whole world. Good and evil suddenly appear in sharp contrast.

David had been meditating on God's love for him. He realized, "Wow! God knows and understands me. God made me. God's pursuing me. God has a plan for me." Then when he wrote, "When I awake, I am still with you" (v. 18), it's as if he came back down to earth. He turned his attention to the world and all the evil he sees prevailing around him. Yes, he was still with God, but he was also in the middle of a mess. That's quite a shock, quite a contrast. We feel the clash anytime we go from meditating on all the lofty truths of God's Word to opening our newspapers or history books filled with the evil that people commit. A painful clash comes when we think of God's marvelous creation and his good purposes contrasted with the destruction, terrorism, and the atrocities people commit toward one another. We are stunned by the global evidences of rampant evil and overwhelmed when it breaks out in our neighborhoods. The holocaust, the killing fields, assassinations, and car bombs may seem like distant theoretical problems until we watch transfixed as airplanes turned bombs destroy mighty structures in our own country. Out of our wounds and grief comes a clearer awareness that there are people all around the world who exploit, who abuse and murder kids, and who commit all sorts of wickedness. When David shifted his attention to the evil in this world and how it destroys the good God desires for so many, he prayed an intense prayer. It's a prayer that expresses hatred for all that is evil and all that casts a dark shadow over the good God intends.

Don't misinterpret his hate as hate toward people; it's hate toward that which degrades and destroys people. This prayer shows David's zeal for God. It's as if David stepped back and said, "Wait a second. There's a lot of competition in my soul for whether I'm going to line up for God's purposes or whether I'm going to line up with the evil influences in the world." Listen carefully. He prayed, "If only you would slay the wicked, O God! Away from me, you bloodthirsty men!" (v. 19). He saw the evil that people can do when they are not living in obedience to God. He saw senseless bloodshed just like in our day, rooted in the selfish ambition that destroys others. David is proclaiming his hate for evil and evil men who, in their quest to satisfy their lusts, utterly reject God's ways. Those who truly meditate on God's intention of creating human beings in his image are all the more zealous against evil that aims to kill, terrorize, and destroy human lives and relationships.

Notice David's loyalty, "Do I not hate those who hate you, O Lord?" (v. 21). He's lining up on God's side, against those who are against God. He says, "Do I not . . . abhor those who rise up against you? I have nothing but hatred for them; I count them my enemies" (vv. 21b–22). His point? David looked at life and said, "There's no room for compromise; I have undivided loyalty to the Lord God of heaven." He saw that there's a cosmic conflict going on against the plan of God in this world. He saw that this world is darkened and warped by wickedness, and he reacted strongly.

We tend to gloss over passages like these. You always hear Psalm 139 quoted, but I can't imagine anyone ever putting verses 19 through 22 on a plaque. But David didn't shy away from the harsh reality that we live in a dark world where real life is warped by wickedness. It is only in light of this reality, as well as the glorious realities seen earlier in Psalm 139, that our disillusionment and discouragement make sense. There's a battle going on between good and evil. Evil in this world fights against and seeks to undermine the truths God laid out in the early part of this psalm. That's why it is so hard for you and for me to see our lives from

God's perspective and to cooperate with his plan for our lives. Every person has to take a stand; we are either part of the solution or we will be sucked in and become part of the problem. Like David, we must learn to ask God to help us see those parts of our hearts and motives that will destroy us if left unattended. So how can we get an accurate view of ourselves in this fallen world?

Search Me

> Search me, O God, and know my heart;
>   test me and know my anxious thoughts.
> See if there is any offensive way in me,
>   and lead me in the way everlasting.
>
> verses 23–24

Verse 23 brings us to the point of personal application. David says, "Search me, O God." He's real honest here. "Know my heart, test me." The word "test" is used in Hebrew to describe the testing of metal to find out if it's pure. "Know my anxious thoughts," literally means "my misgivings." He invited God to examine and point out where he had blown it. "See if there is any offensive way," literally the word for "offensive way" means "way of pain." He was saying, "See if I am following any way that brings about pain." David knew firsthand how easy it to be misled when living in such a darkened world. But he pleas that God would lead him in the everlasting way.

When I feel like a nobody going nowhere, I often pray Psalm 139:23–24 word for word. As God brings things to mind, I confess them and experience his forgiveness and cleansing. It's amazing how a few small sins, bad attitudes, resentments, and little lapses of attention cloud my vision of God and my perception of myself in his eyes.

This World Is in Darkness

God's Word is true, but the darkness of this fallen world influences our perceptions. We don't always live in the light of God's truths: that we are awesome, that God made us, that God values us, that God is pursuing us for our good, and that God has a plan for each of us that will bring us fulfillment. Those truths can look dim when you look at them in light of the influences that surround you. That's why we have to turn on God's light and choose to believe what God says. As we ask God to illuminate our hearts and lead us in the everlasting way, we will have more light to see that we are someone God created with a purpose. When we get farther down that road, we'll be able to see the good God promised develop openly in our lives.

We cannot afford to believe only what we see in this world that is warped by wickedness, because *our perceptions determine our responses.* If we want to respond to God by following his plan and his way, then we must perceive and believe what he says of us more than we believe what appears to be true in this fallen world.

Believe What God Says

A lot of us feel like nobodies because the standard we use for evaluating ourselves is based on standards set by the world. They tell us what's pretty, how our bodies ought to look, how to dress, and what we ought to drive. It's an easy trap to fall into. In every age group, every nationality, every profession, there are worldly standards that tell you how to measure yourself. But that's not how God wants us to live and evaluate ourselves.

In the next section I want to give you some very practical means to win this battle with the world's system. I'd like to share the rest of my story of how God used my time in a tiny town to change my life.

I'd also like to provide some specific help for women who are reading this book. Few areas are as difficult for women to get a grasp of as a "biblical self-image." In the following section I'll briefly share my wife's journey and her amazing progress in an area that seems to be a struggle for nearly all women.

100

EXPERIENCING GOD AS
YOUR LOVING CREATOR

Is This All There Is?

I wandered around Kaufman, Texas, feeling like a nobody going nowhere. What I didn't understand between 1988 and 1990 is that God understood the whole picture. I can see now that God actually allowed me to feel like that. He let me wonder, "Is this all there is?" Those experiences were part of a process. He was refining me, surfacing my motives, and allowing me to reflect on the true source of my significance. He let me consider what gave my life meaning: was it just my accomplishments or was it my acceptance by God? Was my worth dependent on what I did, where I served, how much impact I thought I was making, or was it in the God who made me? Little did I realize then that those deep feelings of insignificance were essential for God to develop what was lacking in me, so that one day he could work more powerfully through me.

God knew what I was going through. He knew what needed to happen in me. All through that difficult process, God was intimately involved in working out his plan for my life. God knows you too. He is orchestrating everything in your life, even the very difficult things. Everything God allows happens for your ultimate benefit. He's on your team. Therefore, he can be trusted. And that trust begins with our accepting by faith that what God has said about us is true.

Do You Like What You See in the Mirror?

Do you get up in the morning, look in the mirror, and say, "Wow, God, what a fantastic person you made. I am unique; I am precious; I don't look like anyone else. I refuse to compare myself to the covers of *Cosmopolitan* and *GQ* and those trivial commercials on TV." Or do you put yourself down as you flip through magazines and compare yourself to the pretty people pictured inside? Do you find yourself watching commercials and wishing you were like someone else? If you are outgoing, do you wish you could be more contemplative? If you are shy, do you wish you were more outgoing? Dissatisfaction seems to be part of human nature. If you have thick hair, you probably wish it was a little thinner. If you don't have any hair, you would take whatever you could get. We spend an inordinate amount of time focusing on what we do not have instead of thanking God for how he has made us.

What Does God Say about You?

One key to enjoying the life God wants you to have is to choose to believe what God says about you instead of what the world implies. I cannot overemphasize how important and pivotal it is that you learn to see yourself as God does! Though critical for all of us, this is especially vital for women who are bombarded daily with the message that their value is based on their outward appearance. But I assure you there is hope. It is possible to develop God's perspective. I have watched my wife do this. I have lived with Theresa for twenty-three years now, known her for twenty-five, and I have seen God change how she views herself.

This wasn't magic. She memorized Psalm 139 and scores of other passages and promises from Scripture that told her who she was in God's eyes. She worked through very difficult views of herself that produced negative feelings. She decided to believe what God declared as true about her, instead of her perceptions of herself as evaluated by the world and as influenced by the baggage and pain of her past. God has transformed her life as he has brought her view of herself into line with his view of her.

It can happen for you, too. It will take hard work. I can remember reviewing flashcards every morning with her in the early years, when a lie she believed was on one side and the truth taught in God's Word was on the other. Because of her steady practice, she literally renewed her mind day after day with God's truth. Over time she began to think and feel dramatically different about herself, the world, and her role. It was a long and arduous journey, but I am now married to a completely different person who finds her acceptance and value in Christ. Although physically beautiful (one biased husband's opinion), her real beauty now radiates from within. She chooses every day to see herself through God's eyes.

You Must Choose

What David points out is that each of us has that choice to make. When you realize that your life is playing out in a sea of conflict, you have to choose where your loyalty lies. It's either going to be lined up with God or it is going to be lined up with the world. David chose to align himself with God. He knew it was easy to get off track, so he asked God to do a check to see if there was anything in his heart that was going along the wicked way. He wanted God to show him, so he could get back on the right track, the everlasting way.

That's what God wants for us. Go ahead and tell God, "I want to be your man (or woman). I want to be a part of the solution, not a part of the problem." Have you made that choice? Right now, choose to align yourself with God and begin to follow him unreservedly. Start today by willfully choosing to radically limit your input of the world's message through the media, and choose to memorize Psalm 139 in order to review how special, valuable, and awesome you are to God.

Someday You Will See the Truth

Remember the scene from *Mr. Holland's Opus*? In that scene Mr. Holland says, "You think that what you do makes a difference, you think it matters to people. Then you wake up one morning, and you find out; well no, you've made a little error." He was chiding himself for making an error in how he perceived his life. And he had, but not in the way he thought. He wasn't seeing the whole picture. He concluded that he had overestimated his value, when the truth was he had underestimated his value. After he cleaned out his desk, his wife and son escorted him into the auditorium where a surprise awaited him. The hall was filled with colleagues, and students—past and present—who had gathered to let him know how much his life had meant to them.

One former student whose life had been significantly impacted by Mr. Holland's life had become the governor of their state. She rose to address Mr. Holland and all those who had gathered to honor his life. She said, "Mr. Holland had a profound influence on my life, on a lot of lives I know. And yet I get the feeling that he considers a great part of his own life misspent. Rumor had it he was always working on this symphony of his. And this was going to make him famous, rich, probably both. But Mr. Holland isn't rich and he isn't famous, at least not outside of our little town. It might be easy for him to think himself a failure. And he would be wrong; because I think he's achieved a success far beyond riches and fame." Then she says to him, "Look around you. There is not a life in this room that you have not touched. And each one of us is a better person because of you. We are your symphony, Mr. Holland. We are the melodies and the notes of your opus, and we are the music of your life."

Not many of us will have such a tribute. But we can learn something from Mr. Holland's experience. Like him, most of us draw conclusions about ourselves in the dim light of the daily grind. We assume that we don't matter, don't make a significant difference; but God says that is not true. Whenever you are inclined to underestimate your value, I urge you to resist that urge. Open the Bible to Psalm 139 and confront your feelings with what God says about you.

Perhaps the following prayer will help you start this process.

Lord, help me not to buy the lie the world hands me. Give me the courage to align my life with you, whatever that means, and to choose to believe what you declare about me rather than what I can see in the light of this dark world. Please show me my purpose in your plan. Help me cooperate with your plan so that it can be fulfilled. Amen.

LIFE LESSONS TO APPLY

1. Remember that God knows you intimately.

2. Remind yourself that God is pursuing you for your good.

3. Remind yourself that God made you—and he says you're awesome!

4. God has a plan just for you. To know it, seek him and cooperate with him fully.

5. Our world is overshadowed by wickedness (which obscures our view of ourselves).

EXPERIENCING GOD WHEN YOU FEEL LIKE A NOBODY GOING NOWHERE

Somewhere you can turn: Psalm 139

KEY VERSES

For you created my inmost being;
you knit me together in my mother's womb.
Your eyes saw my unformed body.
All the days ordained for me
were written in your book
before one of them came to be.
How precious to me are your thoughts, O God!

Psalm 139:13, 16–17a

4

I am with you . . .

WHEN YOU ARE TROUBLED AND DEPRESSED

Christians don't like to admit that they get depressed. Unfortunately, for some believers a stigma is attached to any kind of depression, so they delay acknowledging and dealing with whatever is getting them down. As I prepared the chapters for this book, I asked people from our congregation to share their personal experiences. I had no problem getting volunteers to talk about various areas of difficulty: being paralyzed by fear, getting a raw deal, and blowing it big time. However, when it came to depression, no one volunteered publicly to talk about it even though we had a number of excellent candidates.

People seem to think that if they are walking with God, filled with the Spirit, and making progress as a Christian, they will never wander through the blues. Right? It's not true, but that is the common belief. There's a stigma attached to a Christian who's depressed, isn't there? Some believe it's a sin. Is some depression caused by sin? Sure. Sin causes a lot of things: guilt, depression, lousy relationships, to name just a few; but being depressed is not a sin. If you are normal and you love God, there are going to be days, sometimes weeks, and maybe even seasons when you wrestle with depression. That doesn't mean you are a bad person or an ungodly person; it means you are a real person.

Life Can Get You Down

Life has a way of overwhelming everyone at one time or another. We all have ups and downs. For most of us it's periodic, a little bit down this day or that day, maybe a week or two.

109

Sometimes we even go through a season of grieving deeply or being disheartened after some traumatic loss or stressful life experience. I also realize that some people tend more toward depression—for them the downs are deeper, more complicated. But we all have times when we become disappointed. We struggle. We get mad at people and can't seem to resolve it. We have to juggle demanding schedules, issues of guilt, dependency, problems, and conflicts that leave us feeling emotionally limp. It's no wonder life gets us down. After all, we live in a fallen world.

In this chapter I don't intend to give you a comprehensive look at all the factors that contribute to depression, but I do want you to realize that God isn't surprised or disappointed in you because you are sometimes troubled and depressed. My focus will be on showing you ways God's hand can lift you up and help you out when you are troubled and depressed.

Even Great Leaders and Saints Battle Depression

The author of *Understanding and Coping with Depression* wrote:

Depression is as old as human history. The Bible has many examples of people struggling with despondency and despair. In his depression and fatigue, Elijah asked for his life to be taken. Jonah felt deeply despondent after God did not destroy Nineveh. Jeremiah regretted the day he was born. Job's wife advised him to curse God and die in the midst of the suffering and pain. Well-known church leaders like Martin Luther, John Bunyan, Charles Haddon Spurgeon and J.B. Phillips struggled with depression and so did political leaders such as Winston Churchill and Abraham Lincoln.

Depression is no respecter of persons. It has been called the common cold of emotional disorders and it appears to be on the rise. In the United States it is one of the most prevalent and serious mental disorders, affecting about 20 percent of the population at some time in their lives. People of both genders get depressed, although women are twice as likely as men to suffer from major depressive and dysthymic disorders."[1]

I agree that depression is the common cold of emotional disorders. I also believe that, as with the cold, there is no one cure—not even a spiritual one—that will treat all bouts of depression for all people. Christians often suggest that there is a magic spiritual pill. They may tell you, "Just focus on the Word of God." But when you're depressed, you have no interest in reading the Bible. They may tell you, "Rejoice in the Lord always!" But you can't find any joy—maybe you can't stop crying. They may tell you, "Get up and get moving! Pull yourself out of this. You're being a bad witness. What will people think of God if you, as a professed follower of Christ, look miserable?"

Talk about pressure! Few things are more depressing than having to stop being depressed on command. The person who is down can't help but feel that if they don't snap out of it, they may be condemned. Is it any wonder we hesitate to admit to other Christians that we're depressed?

I Admit It! I've Been Depressed

Since no one else volunteered, I will tell you my own experience. My most severe season of depression occurred in August of 1994. I was about to leave on a pastoral study break after coming through an amazing year. In the fall of 1993 we started holding five services per weekend, and I was preaching in all of them. During the same period, we moved to the local high school to make room for our exploding congregation. We were simultaneously working on a building project, but it hit a snag and came within a few hours of being canceled. On top of everything else, the church went through a financial crisis. We cut staff, cut expenses, but there seemed to be no end to it. The more we cut, the worse it got. Ironically, at the same time, God was doing an amazing work. Scores of people were coming to Christ. In a nutshell, it all added up to the most stressful, fatiguing, difficult period of ministry I'd ever experienced.

I was numb, exhausted, unmotivated, and depressed. I didn't want to do anything. One thought dominated all others—I don't care. Every time we cleared the bar, it felt like it was raised a little higher. There was always another service or another demand on my schedule. Before one season concluded, the next season was on top of us.

When I finally stopped for the study break, I was at a breaking point. I thought, "I don't want to live this way. I don't want to be a pastor. I don't even want to be the person I'm becoming. I don't want to preach. I don't want to do anything." I felt terrible. I was mean and short tempered around my family. My emotions lurked behind a thin veil of self-control. I felt sad and found myself welling up with tears over routine events in my life. I didn't want to talk to anyone. When the phone rang, my first reaction was, "Please don't let it be for me." Ugly!

Then the study break came. I could not study. In fact, I *did* very little. After eleven days of resting and eating and spending time alone with my family, I woke up one morning and sensed a tiny flicker, just a little hint, of joy. It felt so good. I didn't know if there was more where that came from, but I sure hoped so.

Seasons of the Soul and Cries of the Heart

It has been a comfort for me to remember that even the godliest people wrestle with depression on occasion. It is entirely normal for people—even for Christians—to have times when life just gets them down. In the Bible God shows that even great biblical characters were depressed. I am so grateful that God didn't edit out of the Bible the ugly feelings of the writers. He left in their doubts, fears, depressions, despairs, along with their faith. The Book of Psalms reads like an emotional roller coaster. These guys are up, down, up, down, way up, way down. Why? Because they are like us.

Not only does God let us see the emotional seasons of their souls, he also lets us hear their heartfelt cries for help. Then he shows us the many ways he helped them get back up after life knocked them down.

In this chapter, I will walk you through what I believe to be a classic psalm on depression—Psalm 77. It will teach us how to bounce back when we feel least like bouncing at all.

112

God Doesn't Believe in One-Size-Fits-All Solutions

God doesn't offer a magic spiritual potion to cure depression, nor does he offer a one-size-fits-all solution. In fact, God hardly helped any two people out of depression in the same way. God's solutions were related to the person's problem. Consider these brief profiles:

David was extremely depressed while he was keeping his sins of adultery and murder a secret (Psalm 32). God showed up through Nathan to confront the sin and call for repentance. Once that was in motion, God also offered pardon and love—along with expectation of the consequences. When David's son, born of adultery, was ailing, David was depressed and pleaded with God to spare his son's life. When God chose to take the life of the child, as prophesied, David accepted God's judgment, looked forward to seeing the child in eternity, and came out of his despair.

Jonah was depressed because he didn't get his way. The people of Nineveh responded by the thousands to Jonah's message, and that really irritated him because he wanted God to destroy them. He had an attitude problem, which God highlighted with a little object lesson. He first provided shade for Jonah with a fast-growing plant and then took it away. Jonah's depression grew from unresolved bitterness, hatred, and anger because he didn't get his way. God called him to reconsider his view of his own importance and to see those he hated from God's point of view.

Elijah served God with all his might. He was one of the most successful and powerful prophets in the entire Bible. When did he get depressed? At the end of a highly successful campaign where he led the people of God to triumph in a showdown with the evil Queen Jezebel and the prophets of Baal. When that was over, Jezebel threatened him. He collapsed, ran away, and wanted to die. What was God's remedy for him? Angels showed up to make sure he got some good nourishment and a nap!

Job was hit with staggering losses, a prolonged and painful illness, and tortured confusion over why God would let such things happen to him. God didn't give him answers to his questions. Instead, God showed up to question him and give Job a greater view of himself. Then God moved to restore and compensate for much that was lost.

Jeremiah was known as the weeping prophet. He was called by God to take a message to a stubborn, rebellious, and wicked generation of the nation he loved. Jeremiah was obedient to his calling, but when the people he warned got the punishment he predicted, Jeremiah was devastated. How did God help Jeremiah? He let him pour out his broken heart to the Lord and gave him hope. God didn't show up with bolts of lightning, like he did for Job; he didn't recommend a nap; no, with Jeremiah the Lord helped him grasp that which he already believed. Jeremiah wrote, "I remember my affliction and my wandering, the bitterness and the gall. I well remember them, and my soul is downcast within me. Yet this I call to mind and therefore I have hope: Because of the LORD's great love we are not consumed, for his compassions never fail. They are new every morning; great is your faithfulness. I say to myself, 'The LORD is my portion; therefore I will wait for him. The LORD is good to those whose hope is in him, to the one who seeks him; it is good to wait quietly for the salvation of the LORD'" (Lam. 3:19–26).

God's Remedies

God's remedies for these great spiritual men were as varied as the people and situations they faced. Likewise, we should bear in mind that our depressions are often complex too. Even though there is no magical cure for depression, there are scriptural principles that can help.

I have approached the other chapters in this book in roughly three parts: presenting the problem, seeing the problem addressed in Scripture, and then experiencing God's character in the face of that problem. I'm praying and trusting that as you follow the psalmist Asaph through his time of darkness that at some point along the way, God will personally minister to you as he did to the men and women of Scripture.

The life lessons I will offer here are not intended as sequential steps, but as ways God has worked in the lives of others. I know they work more effectively as preventative spiritual maintenance than as depression intervention. I also know that God may use any one of them, or all of them, to bring you out of the fog. Please remember that the reality of God's presence and power doesn't depend on your capacity to feel it or even acknowledge it. When God says, "I am with you always," he means it.

No Ten-Cent Solutions

As I said, depression involves complicated personal issues, and I don't dare give a ten-cent solution for a ten-thousand-dollar problem. Instead, I want to offer you a perspective that will help you see God in every situation. Even though life can be overwhelming and perplexing, God is willing and able to help you sort out the complications in his time. Human troubles, causes and solutions, are varied. We have to have a clear sense of the sources of our trials before we can cooperate with God to find the solutions.

Normal Depression

Sometimes depression or deep sadness represents a normal, even healthy response to the stresses of life. Any one or combination of the following events would make an average person depressed. As you will see, many of experiences on the list are actually positive. These are common stress factors known to contribute to depression:

- Death of a spouse
- Death of immediate family member
- Divorce or separation in your marriage
- Divorce or separation of parents
- Move to a new location
- Addition to your family
- Family member moved away from home

- Completed major goal (such as graduation)
- Loss of job
- New job
- Financial difficulties
- Purchase or sale of a home
- Miscarriage or abortion
- Birth of a baby
- Long work hours
- Pressures and deadlines you are racing to meet
- Physical factors[2]

People also get depressed for proven physical reasons. The human brain is highly sensitive. What may start as an emotional, spiritual, or relational downturn can put such stress on the person that their brain chemistry is affected. When there is a chemical imbalance in the brain, the person experiences mood swings. According to Dr. Paul Meier, "A chemical imbalance in the brain is caused by a depletion or deficiency of neurotransmitters (the chemicals that transmit messages between nerve endings in the brain). This condition at times even requires using antidepressant medication, which has been widely used in recent years with much success. A physician must make the determination and administer the treatment."[3]

Here are some of the physical conditions that contribute to depression:

- Fatigue
- Stress
- Certain kinds of medication: blood pressure medication or over-the-counter cold remedies mixed with other prescription drugs. (If depression comes on without any reasonable explanation, check to see if you have taken any new medications recently.)
- Endocrine imbalance
- Electrolyte imbalance (I have a great friend, a truly spiritual, godly guy who became dehydrated while we were playing

basketball on a mission trip. The guy was in the tank emotionally and spiritually. Come to find out, his whole electrolyte system got out of balance when he became dehydrated. That was the cause of his sudden and severe depression.)

- Diet: low blood sugar levels or hypoglycemia
- Viral infections
- Hormonal changes: typically at puberty, postpartum, and menopause
- Underactive thyroid
- Brain injuries
- Addictions or use of mood-altering drugs or alcohol (This also involves spiritual and psychological factors, but alcohol and many recreational drugs are physical depressants in the body.)[4]

Clinical Depression

When someone is dealing with physiological imbalances (in addition to whatever other factors may have contributed to their initial depression), this is called *clinical depression*. If someone is dealing with clinical depression, they can't get out of it on their own; they will need medical attention. Statistics show that one out of eight people in America will have to have medical treatment for depression at some point in their life.[5]

They may need medication before they can apply other forms of help—including the application of God's Word and counseling. You would probably be surprised at the number of Christians who have been helped by antidepressants at some point in their lives. This is not something Christians openly share with others. Somehow, taking medication that helps the human brain to function properly has been deemed a sin or a lack of faith by some well-meaning Christians. Most people would be shocked if a person broke their arm and decided not to go to the doctor and get it set because they thought it wasn't spiritual to have a broken arm. But when a person gets medical help that addresses the function of the brain, some of those same people see it as a lack of faith. It's not.

Is there a danger that some people might use drugs to avoid pain that they should deal with? Sure. Might some use medication but not deal with other issues that contribute to their depression? Of course. There are dangers involved in many responses to life's problems. But that doesn't mean a person diagnosed with clinical depression doesn't need medical attention to help them get past it. Please understand, we are talking about a very complex issue. Therefore, we need to be careful not to judge others when we don't know what they are dealing with in its entirety. Just because God helped you or someone you know get over depression in one way doesn't mean that is how God always does it or that that is what is necessary in a particular case. It's not one-size-fits-all!

Psychological Factors

There are also psychological reasons people get depressed. Here are some of them:

- A major loss: real or perceived
- Anger that's turned inward
- Guilt: real or imagined
- Major transitions: adolescence, midlife, empty nest, retirement, or other milestones where people tend to evaluate their lives
- Grief
- Faulty and negative thinking
- Being around negative people
- Low self-esteem
- Unrealistic expectations
- Self-pity[6]

118

Finally, there are spiritual factors that can contribute to depression:

- Spiritual exhaustion after a successful ministry (like Elijah)
- Spiritual attack: in 2 Corinthians, Paul talks about all he has come through. He specifically says that he was under spiritual attack. He told how he was so down he wanted to give up until Titus came and refreshed his spirit.
- A wrong perspective (like Jonah)
- Self-effort: trying to do God's work out of the energy of the flesh instead of the power of the Spirit. That can get you depressed (I know a lot about that one).
- Wrong priorities
- Spiritual disappointment (like Jeremiah)
- Spiritual confusion (like Job)
- Rebellion
- Unresolved resentment and bitterness
- Unforgiveness[7]

Depression Affects Body, Mind, and Spirit

Some causes of depression are primarily psychological, some are spiritual, some are physical, and some are relational. During depression, most of these causes overlap, because God made you a whole person. Depression affects the whole being; it's not contained in one psychological compartment. Your spirit, soul, body, and relationships interrelate. When depression touches one area of your life, it affects all the others. That's why there's no one remedy.

So what do you do? I mean biblically, as a Christian who loves God with all your heart, what do you do when you get depressed? Do you deny it? Do you bury it? Do you fake it? Do you have an emotional collapse? Or do you eat more? Watch more TV? Go shopping? Take a vacation you can't afford? Turn to alcohol or drugs? Have an affair? Although I've purposely listed a number of common and often destructive responses to depression, I want

119

you to know that God understands your depression and wants to help you. If you suspect you are clinically depressed and are experiencing serious symptoms that go well beyond occasional dips in motivation and feeling blue, see a quality Christian counselor and/or medical doctor immediately.

The remainder of this chapter is designed to provide biblical counsel and spiritual help for those normal ups and downs that we all face from time to time. In Psalm 77 you will learn a pattern modeled by the psalmist that will help you break out of your feelings of despondency and experience God's power and presence in your life.

PSALM 77

As we look at this portion of Scripture, I don't want you to think, "If I read Psalm 77, no matter what's happening in my life, poof! I will get over my depression." I'm not saying, "Just read Psalm 77 and think the right thoughts, and you will instantly get over being depressed." It's not that easy. I'm not claiming this is a cure for those who are clinically depressed or for those who have a physiological reason for their depression. No, some will need counseling to help them think right before they can begin to pray right. Some may need medical attention. Some may need to repent of sin. There are unique cases and there are people who need specific medical attention, extensive counseling, or both to work through their issues.

But the fact of the matter is, despite all the special circumstances I've described, most depressions are of the common-cold variety. Most people don't necessarily have physical or deep psychological reasons for being depressed. We're not suicidal; we've just lost perspective. What we need is a fresh encounter with God in the midst of the normal struggles we're going through. And that's exactly what Psalm 77 provides.

A Song of Comfort for the Dark Night of the Soul

In Psalm 77 we have a song of comfort for the dark night of the soul. This psalm was written by Asaph. He was Choir Director,

121

one of David's key men, a godly man. His writings give us a pattern to follow to regain our emotional and spiritual equilibrium when life gets us down.

For most of us simply learning to practice what we see in Psalm 77 will help us stay focused during times that might otherwise leave us troubled and depressed. I've noted six life lessons found in this psalm that we can apply at such times.

LIFE LESSON 1: Cry Out to God

> I cried out to God for help;
> I cried out to God to hear me.
> When I was in distress, I sought the Lord;
> at night I stretched out untiring hands
> and my soul refused to be comforted.
>
> I remembered you, O God, and I groaned;
> I mused, and my spirit grew faint.
>
> verses 1–3

An SOS to God

Depression can feel like a cold, dark tunnel, except there isn't any light at the end. If you have ever been in that condition, you know what I mean. Let's hear what the psalmist has to say, "I cried out to God for help; I cried out to God to hear me." The repetition conveys a kind of hopeless sense of calling out in spite of a lack of any confidence that help will come. He's saying, "God, I can't get through." These are cries of distress; nevertheless, he is crying out to God. This is an emotional SOS. "Hey, are you up there? I am hurting down here." He was sleepless, confused, discouraged.

122

Verse 4 goes on, "You kept my eyes from closing; I was too troubled to speak." Have you ever been there? Life can get so confusing; you don't know whether it's anger or depression; it's all mixed up so you can't even speak. You can't figure it out. At those times, just cry out to God, even if all you can do is groan.

God is not put off by your expression of honest, heartfelt emotion. In fact, the Bible promises, "The LORD is close to the brokenhearted and saves those who are crushed in spirit" (Ps. 34:18). Look at the first three verses again and picture what is happening: "I cried out . . . I cried out . . . I stretched out untiring hands . . . I groaned." There is something therapeutic and powerful in simply verbalizing out loud to God what you're feeling. You want to see God show up? You want to have God come close to you? When you feel brokenhearted and crushed in spirit, go ahead and pour out your heartfelt cries to God.

LIFE LESSON 2: Recall Past Blessings

> You kept my eyes from closing;
> I was too troubled to speak.
> I thought about the former days,
> the years of long ago.
> I remembered my songs in the night.
> My heart mused and my spirit inquired.
>
> verses 4–6

As the psalmist lies wide-awake, he lets his mind drift. He thinks, "God must be keeping me from sleep," so he begins to review his personal history. That's the way it is when you're depressed. Often you can't sleep. Your mind runs from subject to subject, trying to make sense of life. Asaph is thinking, "It didn't always used to be this way." He writes, "I remembered my songs in the night." He recalls when God felt near and he could sense his presence. "My heart mused and my spirit

123

inquired." His words strike familiar chords in the hearts of those who have been through the wasteland of depression. They too have said things like, "I don't get it, God. How is it that there were these days when we were so close? I used to feel your joy in my heart. I worshiped with people and I sensed that you were with me, but that seems like a distant dream. Now, you are nowhere to be found." Can you relate? Do you recall feeling like that?

Asaph stopped in the middle of the night, in the midst of his depression, and willed himself to remember God's past blessings. When we don't feel like thinking about anything in particular, we need to have a list of good things in mind upon which we can focus our thoughts. Taking time to recall God's specific blessings in our past provides perspective and peace in the present, especially at times when we are really depressed. Look at how Asaph did it.

Look in the Rearview Mirror

If you are depressed, where does your mind lean? It leans toward how bad it is now; and it's easy to conclude how terrible the future will probably be too. You're thinking, "Life stinks, and it's probably going to get worse. It will never change." You're thinking that person who has been giving you a hard time is a sorry person, and they will always be a sorry person. If you have financial problems, you think they will go on forever. If God doesn't feel near, you think he has left you forever and he'll probably never listen to you again. Isn't that the way our thinking tends to go? You've got to stop that nonsense! You've got to call a mental time-out. You've got to get tough and do a mental turnaround. You've got to look in the rearview mirror and focus on God's past blessings.

Try the Napkin Exercise

I suggest you try what I call "the napkin exercise." I do this often, not every morning, but on more occasions than I would like to admit. I, too, have to deliberately remind myself of my past

blessings. Here's how to do it. Whenever you feel yourself starting to go downhill, put a ballpoint pen in your pocket, go to a
restaurant, get a soda, and pull out a napkin. Begin to list all the
specific blessings that happened that day and that week. These
are facts, not feelings. Don't worry about how you feel about the
blessings. At first you may think there aren't very many. Just try
it. Write down what God has done for you. If you can't think of
anything, start with creation: the sun shining, birds, animals, the
beauty of a flower, white billowy clouds, or any blessing you can
see.

If you have a hard time seeing blessings today, list the best things
that have happened in your life. Look back over the past week or
month and jot down every possibility. If you go blank, look back
over the last year. Cite times God answered your prayers or times
you were protected. If necessary, look back over the last five years.
When you start writing down these blessings, do you know what
you're doing? You are doing what Asaph did to get back up when
life got him down.

Keep a Journal

It has been a valuable discipline for me to keep a journal, and
I recommend you consider giving it a try. I started keeping a
written record of my thoughts, experiences, and prayers a number of years ago, and two things have happened as a result. First,
the writing helps me process and focus as I record my thoughts.
Second, when I start feeling down, I can pull out one of those
journals and review the times I felt up. I have stacks of these
filled notebooks. Now I can open up last week's, last month's,
and show you prayer requests with a check next to what God
did and a date when God did it. By doing this, you will eventually get to the point where you can reread your own stories of
times God met you in the midst of your troubles and lifted you
out of depression. You can remind yourself of what God did.
This is what Asaph did when he wrote, "I will remember the
deeds of the Lord; yes, I will remember your miracles of long
ago. I will meditate on all your works and consider all your
mighty deeds" (vv. 11–12).

125

LIFE LESSON 3: Ask God the Hard Questions

> "Will the Lord reject forever?
>> Will he never show his favor again?
> Has his unfailing love vanished forever?
>> Has his promise failed for all time?
> Has God forgotten to be merciful?
>> Has he in anger withheld his compassion?"
>
> verses 7–9

Asaph asks several searching questions. You may think God wouldn't tolerate such inquiries, but Asaph is sincerely posing the questions that weigh heavily on his heart. We are welcome to do the same. Let's look at the six questions he asks, along with some underlying follow-ups:

- Will the Lord reject forever? Am I going to feel like this forever?
- Will he never show his favor again? Are the good old days always going to be the good old days? Are there never going to be good new days? Am I stuck?
- Has his unfailing love vanished forever? What happened to his covenant love? I don't see it. Has it vanished forever?
- Has his promise failed for all time? Is he not going to do what he said? What I'm going through doesn't seem to be in keeping with God's promises; what's up?
- Has God forgotten to be merciful? In other words, does God have an agenda and somehow I just got off the list? He's taken care of everybody else, but I am over here in need of mercy; did he just forget about me?
- Has he withheld his compassion because he's mad at me? Is that what this is all about? Did I do something wrong? I know I do a lot of things wrong, but is this my punishment?

126

Depression challenges our faith and raises questions. When you get down, really down, do you ask some of these same kinds of questions?

- Where is God?
- Where is this victorious Christian life I've heard so much about?
- Where is the peace and joy?
- Where is the abundant life that God promises and that I've even experienced and have told other people about?
- Where is my faith? I don't feel it anymore; I'm not sure what I believe anymore.

You've probably asked the same questions at one time or another. It is scary to be depressed. Suddenly, you're not sure how your emptiness relates to God and to your standing with him. It's a painful thing. It's deeply confusing. When life gets you down—please take this to heart—*it is normal to ask such questions of God*. Some people are ashamed to admit this kind of inner turmoil, as if voicing such thoughts offends God. I don't think God was offended that Asaph asked his questions. They are included in Holy Scripture. It's as if God wants us to know that we are not alone when we too have such questions. The key thing to remember is to direct your questions to God. Invite him to help you understand what is going on.

LIFE LESSON 4: Choose to Redirect Your Thoughts

> Then I thought, "To this I will appeal:
>   the years of the right hand of the Most High."
> I will remember the deeds of the Lord;
>   yes, I will remember your miracles of long ago.
> I will meditate on all your works
>   and consider all your mighty deeds.
>
>   verses 10–12

Look at the words in this passage that relate to recalling and thinking about the blessings of the past. You may even want to take a pencil or pen and circle the following words: "appeal" (has the idea of thinking back), "remember" (twice), "meditate," and "consider." In these verses, we find five specific verbs that say one simple thing: think back. When life gets us down we need to recall past blessings.

In verse 9 Asaph was questioning God, but notice the shift in his thinking in verse 10, "Then I thought . . ." That's good. Sometimes you've got to think your way out of depression. Sometimes you have to ask yourself, "What would I be thinking about if I wasn't depressed? And then start thinking those thoughts! Asaph did just that when he added, "To this I will appeal: the years of the right hand of the Most High." It's like he's saying, "Here's what I'm going to do; I'm going to look back. I'm going to force my mind back to the years when I saw God doing great things."

Dealing with depression on any level requires an act of the will. You may not be able to control your feelings, but you can choose *not* to give into them entirely. You may not be able to block out depressing thoughts, but you can choose to redirect them to that which is true and uplifting. You can choose to start reading what God has to say to you and applying the lessons he lays out. These positive choices start the process of entering into God's peace, discovering his power, and gaining his perspective in the present circumstance.

Look at how many times the little phrase "I will" is repeated in those verses: "I will appeal," "I will remember," "I will remember," and "I will meditate." These are all choices. When you're going down into what I call the blue funk (you're not totally depressed, but it's coming on), that's when you have important choices to make. Depression is like fog coming in over the ocean. You can see it creeping in. It's not where you are yet; but you are looking out and you can see it coming in. If you stay where you are, you are going to be enveloped in the fog.

That's how the blue funk invades my mind and emotions. I have a low feeling, a little energy loss, a couple of negative thoughts, and I start to think, "Life is beginning to stink." During those times, I don't like me; and if you happen to call just about then, I don't like you either. My family watches as I shift from upbeat to critical, from positive to negative. I can feel my emotions sinking.

When the blue funk is creeping up on me, that's when I have a choice to make. Will I choose to fight the battle or just stay inactive and let it envelop me? I can't document this, but it seems to me that there's a secret, weird part of my psyche that wants to just let myself sink. My thinking goes like this: "I see a down time coming. I don't want to allow it, but I think I will." You know what I'm saying? In a warped, self-centered kind of way, it seems like it will be good to feel bad. Why? Because if I'm depressed, everyone will pity me. But as I begin to feel this way, I realize there's a rope still within my reach, and I better grab it. That reaching for the rope has everything to do with exercising your will.

Making Good Choices Leads to Good Feelings

I remember vividly what it was like in the tank of depression. I understood that reading the Bible and applying its principles would help me, but I didn't want to read the Bible. When you are a pastor and you are on a study break to study the Bible, but that's the last thing you want to do, you've got a problem. I didn't want to pray either. It was not a real good situation. So I asked myself, "What are you going to do?" I remember telling God, "I need to be reconnected with you." Who wants a pastor preaching sermons that don't come from a sincere heart? Then I made a decision. I said, "God, I am going to read through the Psalms. I don't feel like doing it; I don't want to do it; I *choose* to do it."

The first day I read a psalm or two and the little phrase "your unfailing love" caught my attention. I said to God, "All I am going to do is read and see how many times *'your unfailing love'* shows up. I'm going to highlight it, circle it, read, and reread about your unfailing love. I'm going to try to learn what David and the other psalmists knew about it." But remember, though I recognized these were precious words, I didn't feel what they were describing. So I prayed, "God, the Bible says that your

129

covenant love is unconditional. It says that when I am a jerk, you love me. When I am doing well, you love me; it says your love never fails. So, even though I don't feel it—I don't even know if I believe it right now—I nevertheless choose to focus on your unfailing love."

I started reading. I saw how he was faithful to other people who struggled. I did that for ten days and felt no better. Then sometime during day eleven, a little light came on. My feelings began to change. Notice the progression: I chose to do something I knew was good without feeling like it, I persisted, and then my feelings caught up with my good choice.

LIFE LESSON 5: Magnify God to Diminish Your Problems

When we are depressed, molehills grow into mountains. It's all a matter of perspective. If you hold a little problem very close, and you focus on that, what do you see? You see everything through the lens of that problem. The psalmist demonstrates how you can pull back and get perspective. This is essential, because depression often involves a loss of hope. When your problems loom large and God seems distant, your hope of successfully dealing with that overwhelming problem is dim. Before you can have hope you have to rediscover that God is a *big* God and any problem is small in comparison. That renews your hope and lifts your spirits. Notice Asaph's focus beginning in verse 13.

Magnify God as the Most High

> Your ways, O God, are holy.
>> What god is so great as our God?
> You are the God who performs miracles;
>> you display your power among the peoples.
> With your mighty arm you redeemed your people,
>> the descendants of Jacob and Joseph.

> The waters saw you, O God,
> the waters saw you and writhed;
> the very depths were convulsed.
> The clouds poured down water,
> the skies resounded with thunder;
> your arrows flashed back and forth.
> Your thunder was heard in the whirlwind,
> your lightning lit up the world;
> the earth trembled and quaked.
>
> verses 13–18

Seeing a Big God

Asaph used an interesting Hebrew phrase for God that literally means "God, the Most High." The ancient name is *El Elyon*. It's a name that refers to God as the Creator and protector of the universe. Asaph reminded himself that this isn't just a god, it is *the* God, Most High. This was written at a time when the Hebrew people lived among other nations who worshiped Canaanite deities. People were always fighting over whose god was the most powerful or most high.

Baal was known as the Canaanite god of the sea, thunder, and storm. Asaph asserts that the God of the Hebrews is superior to other gods. Having made that claim, Asaph states, "The waters saw you, O God, the waters saw you and writhed; the very depths were convulsed. The clouds poured down water, the skies resounded with thunder; your arrows flashed back and forth. Your thunder was heard in the whirlwind, your lightning lit up the world; the earth trembled and quaked." He reminded himself that the God to whom he appealed is in charge of all nature and superior to any so-called deity.

After concentrating his attention on God's mighty acts, Asaph then shifted his focus to God's ways. There's a progression: focusing on God's acts leads to remembering his ways, which then reveals his character. The result will be a change of perspective. Look at it with me. Asaph said, "Your ways, O God, are holy. What god is so great as our God?" Does that sound like our buddy

131

Asaph was still depressed? Where did he get his new perspective? He got it because he recited all those great acts of God. The word "holy" in this passage means "above reproach, in unapproachable light." More than one commentator has noted that God's holiness makes him such a formidable foe that any enemy would run. Think of it, when we see God as holy and realize that he is on our side, it has a way of putting whatever is getting us down into that perspective.

Asaph went on, "You are the God who performs miracles." He reminded himself that God is not only holy, but great and powerful. He reminded himself of all the times God's people needed a miracle and God provided amazing help. He reasoned within himself, "God, you have done it before; therefore, you can do it again." He wrote, "You display your power among the peoples, with your mighty arm you redeemed your people, the descendants of Jacob and Joseph." Notice the three characteristics of God's nature that Asaph mentions: (1) God is holy; (2) God does miracles, showing he's powerful; (3) God redeems his people, demonstrating he cares and loves. The Hebrew word for "redeem" refers to a special relationship in that culture called the "kinsman redeemer." It's a picture of God saying, "I care for you. We're spiritually blood relatives. I care about your situation and I will pull you out of it."

Big Problem, Little God or Big God, Little Problem

Asaph began with a huge problem and a tiny God; but when he changed his perspective to see God as *big*, his problems faded into the background. Here's how it works. As long as we focus on our problems, they loom large. If you have a really *big* problem that overwhelms you to the point of depression, it indicates that you see God as small. Once you change your perspective, you can see that you have a tiny problem. See, you've got to go one way or the other.

I don't know what you are facing, but it is a very small problem to God, who created the heavens, the earth, the seas, and everything else; who sustains the universe by the word of his power; and who raised the dead. Scripture says that the purposes of God will not be thwarted. He is in charge of the world, and he's in charge of your world. When you really believe that and focus your attention on how holy, powerful, and caring God is; you will literally see your problem shrink. You may not get there right away. But if you stop, choose to look at his acts, and then begin to see his ways, you will eventually perceive his character. You will see that he is *big*, he's powerful, and he's concerned about you!

LIFE LESSON 6: Trust God to Be Your Deliverer

> Your path led through the sea,
>   your way through the mighty waters,
>   though your footprints were not seen.
>
> You led your people like a flock
>   by the hand of Moses and Aaron.
>
> verses 19–20

Asaph refers to one of God's greatest acts of power on behalf of his people. It's a reference that Israel makes every time they are in need. What is it? It's the time God parted the Red Sea and delivered the people of Israel from slavery in Egypt. God heard their cries and saved them from their powerful enemies. It was an impossible situation. They were probably thinking, "We're going to die! We're all going to die—now!" But God met them in the midst of their greatest troubles and they didn't die. God led them on a path through the sea and out of slavery. There seemed no way out, but God showed up as their mighty Deliverer and he made a way out for them. If you can't remember times God delivered you personally, rent the video *The Ten Commandments* or *Prince of Egypt* and remind yourself that the God you are praying to is the same God who parted the Red Sea, and he can part your Red Sea.

133

There Is a Way Out

When we're depressed, we think that there's no way out. But the psalmist says, "That's not true. That's not true historically. That's not true theologically. That is not true for me and it's not true for you." Even though the people of Israel never saw his footprints, God was there. He delivered Israel in a miraculous and spectacular way. In those times when you don't feel close to God, and it looks like there is no way out; there is still a way out. God is invisible, but he is with you and he will deliver you.

Notice Asaph adds that God leads as a shepherd. A shepherd treats his flock with wisdom, tenderness, and care. That means God will never give you more than you can handle. God will show up when you need him and when you cry out to him. God does the miraculous, but it's not always accomplished by supernatural means. Sometimes God shows up to deliver you through people. Even though God led his people miraculously through the sea, he still used people. He led them by the hand of Moses and Aaron.

You see, God is a shepherd who cares for each person individually. Even though you might not be able to sort out all the contributing factors to your depression, God can still lead you out of it. He will lead you to the help you need: it may involve medicine, counseling, spiritual direction, relational aid, or all of the above. But God wants to meet you in the midst of your troubles and depression and lead you out.

In the following section, I have put together some specific tools to help you put into practice the truth of Psalm 77. Depression is debilitating; don't stop here! Read the next few pages to discern what specific action steps God would have you *choose* to take to allow him to part the Red Sea of your depression.

Experiencing God as the Lifter of Your Soul

So, where do we go from here? We've learned depression is normal, like the common cold. We'll face our bouts with this dark night of the soul. And though we've been quick to point out that there are no magic pills or spiritual formulas to pull us out of our times of despair, God has provided some powerful and timeless principles in Psalm 77 to help us do battle when those listless feelings of dread and discouragement seek to lure us into despondency.

With that in view, allow me to take the truth we've learned and put it into the form of some diagnostic questions that will help you discern how to respond in your particular situation. I'd like to arrange these questions in three distinct categories that have been of great value to me over the years. In fact, I've developed a personal action plan from Psalm 77 that I use whenever the blue funk of depression begins to descend upon me.

An Action Plan to Overcome Depression

Examine Your Thinking

Do you recognize that it is *normal* to feel depressed now and then? It may sound like I'm restating the obvious, but this is the first question I ask myself. Why? Because I tend to immediately think something very terrible or very wrong is happening to me. Despite physical fatigue, major trauma, or great loss—all of which will bring on at least mild forms of depression—I tend to assume I'm a bad person, I must have sinned somehow, or my priorities must be totally out of line. The moment I ask the above question, I'm reminded that depression may well be God's way of slowing me down or insulating my emotions in a time of crisis, or it may simply be normal after the stress, pressure, and intensity of a highly important time of ministry.

Is your focus on the pressure/problems you're experiencing, or on your response to those pressures/problems?

On the surface it may seem like there's not a lot of difference, but I assure you it makes all the difference in the world. As long as we *focus* on the problems, they grow. But the moment we begin to focus on *our response* to the problems, we gain a whole new level of self-awareness. We move from being a victim upon whom all these terrible things/feelings are piling up on, to being a chooser who has the power and responsibility to deal with them positively or negatively. This small shift in focus is when we move from having big problems and a small God to having a big God and small problems.

Examine Your Behavior

Are you choosing positive or negative responses to your depression?

Because depression involves a battle of the will, it is crucial to objectively ask and answer what your behavior is indicating about your response to depression. If you are slipping into escapism behavior that involves TV, food, procrastination, excessive sleep, drugs, alcohol, or pornography, you know immediately that you are on a downward spiral, allowing the depression to take an even deeper place in your soul. Guilt will follow such behaviors, which in turn will reinforce your already negative thoughts and feelings about yourself, which leads to even more negative behavior, which . . . you get the idea.

That's why when you read the above question you must make a quick and immediate choice! You must choose regardless of your feelings to engage in positive behavior ASAP! It doesn't even have to be spiritual, but you must *act!* You simply can't afford to continue the negative introspection and behavior. The following list represents a variety of *positive actions* I've used and continue to use as I feel myself sinking into a depression.

- Get a workout
- Take a walk
- Write a letter
- Call someone who's ill or struggling
- Write out my prayers
- Listen to uplifting music
- Go visit a good friend
- Listen to a sermon or book on tape
- Randomly visit people in the hospital (even if I don't know them)
- Read the Bible

Getting active in some positive behavior tends to at least put the brakes on depression. Now it is time to refocus your thinking and renew your perspective.

Recall God's Blessings

Have you *willfully stopped* to recall God's blessings in your life?

I know it may sound a little trite, but few things reshape and restore our perspective more than this. Asaph modeled this in Psalm 77. David commands it in Psalm 103. Jesus instituted it as a regular practice for his church when he turned the Passover into the Lord's Supper as a memorial of his love and sacrifice for us. "Do this in *remembrance* of me."

So, if you're feeling blue and struggling with depression, I want you to stop right now and reflect on God's blessings and good-

137

ness. Yes, I know you don't feel like it. I didn't ask you to feel like it. I asked you to do it! Take some time right now and

- Get out those photo albums
- Look at wedding pictures
- Remember good moments with shots of the kids
- Reminisce with favorite vacation pictures
- Look at birthday pictures
- Revisit slides
- Watch old videos you haven't watched in years
- Read your journal
- Do the napkin exercise
- Relive the day you came to Christ
- List the top ten answers to prayer in your life
- List five people who love you

You may think I'm crazy or this is silly, but you will be shocked at the power of reviewing God's blessings. After I taught this in our church, one man said he thought it was one of the dumbest things he'd ever heard but was so depressed he went ahead and tried it anyway. He beamed as he told me how deeply God spoke to him as he walked through and reviewed wedding pictures with his wife the previous day. Go ahead and break out those old pictures. You'll be glad you did.

Examine Your Future

Can the God *who did so much in your past* handle what you're facing today? Read that question out loud! Of course you know the answer intellectually, but it's crucial to confront your emotions and warped perspective with the truth. I mean ask yourself, "Have I ever been depressed before?" "Did I come out of it, or did the world come to an end?" After examining your thinking and behavior, it is extremely helpful to begin looking toward the future. When we're depressed, we falsely believe the future is bad, negative, and hopeless. But the truth is *today is not the worst day in your life.* God has brought you and others through a lot worse than what you're facing today, and he is able and committed to taking you through tomorrow.

Help Someone Else

Is there a *specific, positive step* you could take to *help someone else* in order to demonstrate your confidence in God's love for you? This question may sound unrelated to depression, but it's not. You see, depression not only makes the future seem bleak, it has this *insidious and ugly by-product of having us put all our attention and focus on ourselves.* We become ungrateful in our upward focus with God, negative in our inward focus with ourselves, and insensitive in our outward focus toward others.

I remember reading somewhere the account of an acutely depressed man who had been treated in every manner possible without success. As a last resort, the head of the hospital staff sent the man on an errand, explaining to him no one was available to help the doctor, and he desperately needed this man's help. He sent him to deliver words of encouragement to another man in the hospital, a man dying of terminal cancer. That event marked the beginning of his victory over depression as his focus moved from himself to the needs of someone else.

So why not ask yourself, or better yet, ask God who right now might need a word of encouragement, an hour of time, a ride to the airport, a bag of groceries, or a phone call from you.

Isn't it great to know that God invites us through Psalm 77 to experience God as the lifter of our souls when we're depressed. When we remember his acts, remember his ways, and remember that he is Most High, we gain perspective. We serve a *big* God who can dwarf any problem we bring to him—even if we brought it on ourselves. Remind yourself that God is a deliverer. He delivered his people in the past. Therefore, what will he do? He will deliver you in the future.

LIFE LESSONS TO APPLY

1. Cry out to God; pour out your heartfelt emotions.

2. Stop to remember and recall past blessings and times God delivered you from your troubles.

3. Ask God the questions that are weighing on your heart.

4. Choose to redirect your thoughts rather than give in to your feelings.

5. Magnify God to diminish your problems.

6. Trust in God to be your deliverer from troubles and to help you recover from depression according to your specific situation and condition.

EXPERIENCING GOD WHEN YOU ARE TROUBLED AND DEPRESSED

Somewhere you can turn: Psalm 77

KEY VERSES

You are the God who performs miracles;
you display your power among the peoples.
With your mighty arm you redeemed your people,
the descendants of Jacob and Joseph.

Psalm 77:14–15

140

I am with you . . .

WHEN YOU ARE GRIPPED BY FEAR

I have a little note written in green ink next to Psalm 46 in the margin of my Bible. It says, "Duke Medical Center, 2/19/92." Then, in parentheses, "Mom's dying." Next to it, highlighted in green, are these words from the psalm: "God is our refuge and strength, an ever-present help in trouble. Therefore, we will not fear, though the earth give way and the mountains fall into the heart of the sea, though the waters roar and foam and the mountains quake with their surging." That note brings back sharp memories and deep feelings. I remember writing it. I distinctly remember our room at the Brown Shoe Inn, where my family took up temporary residence. And I remember what brought us together.

My mom had gone in for a routine check-up to get a second opinion concerning her prolonged battle with a rare blood disease related to Lupus. She had taken an overnight bag for her brief flight from Florida and the one day of scheduled tests. These were just "routine," let's-get-a-second-opinion tests. She had no idea she would never come home.

My Life Took a Terrifying Turn

Two days later I got a call—you know how it goes—the news instantly jumbled my world. The words were medical terms, but they reached deep inside me. I was gripped by fear. They told me my mother had a systemic infection in her blood. I caught the first flight and found myself at Duke Medical Center in the wee hours of the morning.

We did what families do. We gathered together and waited in a little room next to the ICU. Before long, we knew Mom's condition was rapidly deteriorating, more frightful with each report. Suddenly, doctors were jarring us with talk about amputating limbs to save her life. But even that desperate option was removed when they had to quickly put her on life support. Hope seemed to drain out of us as we began to discuss and try to figure out whether to pull the plug, when, and why.

What started out as an ordinary week took an unexpected, wrenching, and terrifying turn. You know what that's like, don't you? Times when you have to deal with issues that you haven't even thought about until then. Life doesn't respect our reluctance or allow us to escape for long. Life doesn't seem to care that we don't want to face a key family member's death. What we fear and avoid comes anyway.

My mom was the glue of our family; she held everything and everyone together. We couldn't begin to imagine her gone. Yet, as we sat there in stunned quietness—siblings, extended family, and our father—we had to begin to talk about life and death issues we'd never dealt with in all the years we'd been a family.

Where Was God?

I needed God. I had never needed him more. That note in the margin of my Bible reminds me of that time when Psalm 46 became the anchor of my soul. As I read those words in that terrifying setting, I experienced God. I experienced more of God during those days surrounding my mother's death in 1992 than I had ever experienced of him up to that point in my life. He became, in an unforgettable way, my refuge, providing protection, internal strength; and power to endure moment by moment. He provided me—in the midst of fear-filled adversity—with a continual flow of grace and peace. He was a very, very present help in my time of trouble. I sensed his presence in extraordinary ways. He was available—right there. He was even a source of unexpected joy that somehow made its way into one of the worst times of my life, bringing a sense of confidence that no matter what, even in the face of death—perhaps, especially in the face of death—God can reveal himself.

What I experienced while my mother was dying is what God desires all of his children to experience when we're paralyzed or overwhelmed by fear. We have his Word on it. Psalm 46 is a classic portion of Scripture to turn to whenever fear grips our hearts.

Let me be as abrupt as life for a moment: If I handed you one of those dry-erase markers and a white-board and asked you to write down your greatest fear, what would you write? What causes your chest to tighten and your stomach to churn? What person, situation, or future event do you dread? What fears do you have whose source you can't even identify? We all have fear. In fact, we don't have to look for fear; it finds us.

Fear

What do we mean by *fear?* One dictionary defines fear as a sudden attack, anxiety, or agitation caused by the presence or nearness of danger, evil, or pain. It covers a range of emotions: timidity, apprehension, terror, dread. But most of us don't need a dictionary to tell us what fear is; we know it in far more personal terms. Some of us are gripped by fear when we think about our loved ones; for others, it's when we think about the future. Some have fears concerning their marriage. Others are afraid they'll never get married. Some have fears of being alone; others have fears of the dark. Maybe you struggle with panic attacks and no one knows it. Maybe you hate crowds and are overwhelmed by fear in public places. You may be fearful of loneliness; so when everyone leaves, you keep the television on for company. That doesn't always work, because the news of terrorist attacks, biochemical dangers, and nuclear threats can set off a whole series of fearful thoughts. You may have financial fears or job fears. You may have fears about aging parents, or about your kids and how they're going to turn out, and who they're running around with. You may have fears about how you'll pay the bills. You may have fears about retirement and about where you're going to live and

145

if you can continue to afford your lifestyle. There's no shortage of things that can grip our hearts with fear.

The C-Word

The word "cancer" is enough to strike fear in most any heart, a word that can turn your world upside down in a moment. Even though medical science has found effective ways to deal with that dread disease, it still is frightful. That's especially so because it can strike six- and eight-year-olds, as well as sixty-eight-year-olds. Being a parent, I can't think of many things more frightful than to hear the doctor say, "Your child has cancer." But that's what happened to Carl and Phyllis Biggs with their twenty-two-year-old son, John.

I know this family from our church very well. I was very close to John, his parents, and his fiancée, Christine. John began to have some nagging medical problems. The doctors couldn't figure out what was wrong. They did gastro-intestinal tests and put him through the whole battery of other diagnostic tools that modern medicine has in its arsenal, but they couldn't determine the problem. Then the symptoms worsened, and the cause became apparent. I was called with the news that John had cancer. I hopped in my car and headed over to Dominican Hospital to meet with them.

I did what I expect you would do in that situation. As I drove, I thought, "What do I say to a mom and dad—let alone a twenty-two-year-old young man—who have just found out he has cancer?" At that point they didn't know exactly what kind; they didn't know the implications. They didn't know if it was one of those cancers with a high cure rate or if he only had months to live. But imagine yourself in a hospital room, looking at your child who has just been diagnosed with cancer. Imagine all the dreams you would be reconsidering, wondering if your child would ever get a chance to play outside. How would you think of the future with such a looming dark cloud on the horizon? Imagine the impact to your family and how your schedule would come to a screeching halt.

146

So, as I drove, I prayed, "Lord, what do I say? I don't have any resources that can help them, but I know you do. What could you give me that I could give to them?" I didn't want to give them just words; I wanted to bring them something that would allow them to experience God. I walked in the room and we had some nervous chitchat followed by some quiet moments talking about the situation. Then I sat on the edge of the bed and I opened up my Bible to Psalm 46.

PSALM 46

A Song against Fear

Psalm 46 is a song of hope and confidence. Like any good song, it's composed in verses or stanzas. You might notice the little word *Selah* in between each stanza. *Selah* is a musical term telling the singer to pause; but it's more than that. It's also a note to the readers or listeners, directing us to stop after each verse in order to reflect on each separate idea or picture the psalmist paints in that stanza. Let's look at each section to get an overview of what God wants us to see.

The first stanza (vv. 1–3) tells us *what:* God is our refuge, our source of hope in times of trouble. The second stanza (vv. 4–7) tells us *why:* God's presence is our sure reason for hope. The third, and last, stanza (vv. 8–11) tells us *how:* we can experience God's presence, even in our most troubled times. But before we look at each stanza, I'd like you to take a moment to notice a key theme of the psalm.

God Is for Us!

Throughout all three stanzas one phrase is repeated. It's as if God wants to underscore a very important point for us. It's a crucial little phrase that gets lost in some translations. We can't afford

148

to lose it. It's found in verses 1, 7, and 11. In verse 1, what reads, "God is our refuge and strength" would literally read, "God is *for us*, a refuge and strength *for us*." Verse 7 would literally read, "The God of Jacob is *for us* a fortress." Verse 11 would literally read, "The Lord of hosts is *for us*." The point the repetition of this little phrase emphasizes is that we do not have to be afraid because God is *for us*.

God wants you to know that he is for you. He is on your side. He is not waiting for you to mess up. When you're in trouble and you realize that you brought 80 percent of it on yourself, God doesn't have his arms crossed with a smirk on his face as if to say, "*See, ha! ha! ha! I knew you would fail!*" That's a picture of God some carry with them from childhood, but it's not a biblical one. God is for you; he is not against you. That may be hard for you to grasp, but it is central to experiencing God when you're gripped by fear.

Maybe you're familiar with the great old hymn *A Mighty Fortress Is Our God*, penned by Martin Luther, the German reformer. Even though he composed it around the year 1529, that hymn is still sung today in many churches. It is timeless because it communicates a powerful truth needed in every generation. Psalm 46 inspired Luther to write those lyrics. How comforting to know that God is our mighty fortress. But there is one line in the hymn that highlights the recurrent theme that God is for us. That line says, "*That Word above all earthly pow'rs, no thanks to them, abideth; The Spirit and the gifts are ours through Him who with us sideth.*" Martin Luther clearly expressed his realization that God was on his side. Perhaps that goes a long way toward explaining how he could confront the political and corrupt religious powers of his day without being gripped or held back by fear. You can have that same kind of hope and confidence; you can have that same experience of the presence of God when you are afraid.

Let me ask you this: How differently would you face your greatest fears if you believed that God was on your side? Call to mind that fear you wrote on the imaginary white-board, then as we go through the lessons of each stanza, ask God to help you apply what it says to your own heart and mind.

God Is Our Refuge

> God is our refuge and strength,
>   an ever-present help in trouble.
> Therefore we will not fear, though the earth give way
>   and the mountains fall into the heart of the sea,
> though its waters roar and foam
>   and the mountains quake with their surging. *Selah*
>
> verses 1–3

The first three verses talk about God, our source of hope. In the face of trouble, God is our place of safety, our source of power, and our constant helper. That's who he is. Since that's true, "Therefore we will not fear." And now, get this. The writer takes the two most indestructible, stable things imaginable, and by way of hyperbole says, "If all the pillars in your life, if all the things that you know you can count on are removed, it doesn't matter because God is consistent." "Therefore, though the *earth give way* and the *mountains would fall into the heart of the sea,* and though its waters roar and foam and the mountains quake with their surging," what's he saying? God and God alone is your only security. That's the theme. God is our source. *Here's the life lesson: We don't have to be afraid, because God can handle even the worst imaginable scenario.*

God wants to support you in three ways.

First, God is a refuge. A refuge is a defensive place of protection. Refuge refers to the external issues of life. A refuge is a place where you can run, and find safety. God says he is for you. He wants to be your refuge. He will be a refuge. Not a big steel building. Not some cave dug out of solid rock and filled with survival food. Much bigger than that. The God of the universe says, "I personally will be your refuge. You can come in to me and I will wrap my arms around you and I won't let anything touch you. I will be for you a refuge."

Second, God will be for you a strength. This is an internal provision. This is the power to endure. God only gives strength for the moment, moment by moment. He is not strength for tomorrow

150

until tomorrow. Unfortunately, we all tend to worry about tomorrow. What about the job tomorrow? What if this relationship goes sour in a month? What if I don't have . . . ? We get anxious the moment we begin projecting into the future. We get all uptight and fearful. Do you know why? Because we're getting ahead of life. We're forgetting Jesus' words about worry, "Therefore do not worry about tomorrow, for tomorrow will worry about itself. Each day has enough trouble of its own" (Matt. 6:34).

There is no such thing as hypothetical grace. There is no grace provided a day in advance; no tomorrow's grace today. God only provides grace for this moment—and that's more than enough, considering the source. How do you know tomorrow is even coming? Our only responsibility is to trust God for today. And God promises he will be your strength in the moment you need it. If you need "x amount" of grace to make it through this hour, that's how much grace you get. If in the next hour it gets tougher and you need much more grace, that's how much more grace you will get. Moment by moment, God will be for you strength.

Third, God is for you an ever-present or very present help. When? In times of trouble. It means he is readily available during the trouble, no matter how unexpected, no matter how hard, and no matter how overwhelming. You can experience God with you whenever you're in trouble. Look at the imagery of the waters used here. Picture an ocean surging in a tumultuous hurricane. The waters "roar and foam." It is dangerous and forceful. The waters are raging; they are chaotic and unstable. Even at times like that, God is right there with you in the stormy waters.

The psalmist's words bring to mind the picture of Jesus asleep in a boat on the Sea of Galilee. The waters were suddenly churned up. The disciples were terrified, screaming that they were all going to die. But Jesus was right there in the same boat with them. He was their present help in their time of trouble. And God is in the same boat with you when you find yourself in stormy waters. In fact, the next stanza describes how God's presence gives us hope in the midst of our trouble.

151

God's Presence Gives Us Hope

> There is a river whose streams make glad the city of God,
> the holy place where the Most High dwells.
> God is within her, she will not fall;
> God will help her at break of day.
> Nations are in uproar, kingdoms fall;
> he lifts his voice, the earth melts.
>
> The LORD Almighty is with us;
> the God of Jacob is our fortress. *Selah*
>
> verses 4–7

The message of this stanza is that in the midst of trouble—no matter how cataclysmic—God's presence can be like a river that flows from the very heart of God. That river brings all God's infinite resources to his people, flowing down into the place where they are protected, where there is unlimited supply of whatever they need, where God will back them with his forces and resources. I want you to see that God is promising the same to you in whatever frightful situation you may find yourself.

Okay, maybe you're thinking, "Chip, where do you get this stuff? It sounds great, but how did you get all that from those verses? I didn't see anything about an unlimited supply of joy, protection, deliverance, security? Where did you get that?" Let me show you.

Old Testament Images

The writer was using Old Testament imagery, so we have to understand something of what these images meant to the people of that day. When you understand what the imagery meant to the original audience, you will see better how it applies to you. Here are the elements of the imagery that have significance.

The city of God refers to Jerusalem. Historically, Jerusalem wasn't just a city that David, King of Israel, picked out because he thought, "This would be a nice place for a capital." It was a strategic decision. People talk about going *up* to Jerusalem because the city itself is situated on a high place. Even if I hadn't known of the city's importance when I saw it myself, I would have been impressed by its appearance. It is like a fortress. Below stand the pillars and walls of rock going up and up, and then, high above, rests the city. And Jerusalem herself has huge walls all around, where the sentries guarded the city.

An adequate fortress city not only had to be elevated and protected by strong walls, it also had to have a source of fresh water. The river of Siloam flows into Jerusalem. Great cities in ancient times endured battle after battle. Sieges sometimes lasted years. The aim was to have a fortress that your enemy couldn't overrun. One of the inherent weaknesses of walled cities, even if they were great fortresses, was their water supply. If you had a fresh water supply and plenty of food, you could stay in there indefinitely.

So, for an Israelite in that day, Psalm 46 produced the following mental picture with which he could relate immediately: There's a mighty fortress city, surrounded by outward opposition, danger, and a determined enemy. Beyond the walls, the battle is fierce. But even while all that's happening on the outside, a stream continues to flow into the besieged fortress city. No wonder it's a river whose streams make glad the city of God. With that picture of supply, even through the battle was raging all around, it was safe in the city of God because they had a source of water.

The waters in Jerusalem flow from the Gihon spring to the Pool of Siloam and are called the waters of Shiloah. In this desert, where a supply of fresh water can mean the difference between death and life, a stream of water that makes glad the city of God symbolized the sustaining power of the Lord.

Notice the contrast between the waters mentioned in verse four and those in verse three. Those were dangerous waves; these are life-giving waters. We see the same kind of contrast in Isaiah, chapter 8, where God said his people rejected the "gently flowing waters of Shiloah"—referring to how people of Israel had rejected God's protection. Instead of taking refuge in God, they looked to other countries to protect them. God warned that because of their rejection of his sustaining power, they would be overtaken by "mighty floodwaters" symbolizing the Assyrian army. But even in those words of doom, God expressed his desire to be their refuge in their coming time of trouble. He called himself Immanuel, which means, "God with us."

The biblical imagery also refers to being in God's very presence, not just in the imagery of the earthly Jerusalem, but in the heavenly Jerusalem. The earthly Jerusalem is said to be but a replica of the city of God in heaven. Revelation 22:1 says, "Then the angel showed me the river of the water of life, as clear as crystal, flowing from the throne of God and of the Lamb down the middle of the great street of the city. On each side of the river stood the tree of life, bearing twelve crops of fruit, yielding its fruit every month. And the leaves of the tree are for the healing of the nations. No longer will there be any curse. The throne of God and of the Lamb will be in the city, and his servants will serve him" (Rev. 22:1–3).

Both Psalm 46 and the passage from Revelation speak of gaining sustenance from the very throne of God. And guess what flows from the throne of God that gives life? A river. So here we see the connection between God's presence and his sustaining provision—not only for this life, but even crossing over into eternity. Not only is God providing his presence; God is committed to help! And when you have God on your side, whom else do you need?

These verses show us his power. Even though the nations are in an uproar and kingdoms fall, God lifts his voice and the earth melts. God has the power to help you—even if your whole world is coming down all around you. The political world around you may be in as much turmoil as the emotional world within you. God is a present help for both.

"The Lord Almighty is with us," declares the end of the second stanza. "The Lord Almighty" could be translated literally, "the Lord of Hosts." The terms evoke military imagery—the Lord with all of his armies and all of his resources. So, who is with us? God, in full force, leading all the armies of heaven. To the Hebrew mind this might recall the time the prophet Elisha and his servant were surrounded by enemy forces (2 Kings 6:8–17). The servant was terrified, and understandably so. Then Elisha prayed, "O Lord, open his eyes so he may see." Then the Lord opened the servant's eyes, and he looked and saw the hills covered with heavenly warriors, horses, and chariots of fire all around Elisha. That same Lord Almighty who stationed invisible armies all around Elisha will be with you when you're in trouble, and he will bring all his mighty forces with him. Do you suppose the servant's fear level dropped when he saw the forces that were arrayed on his side? It's the same for us. And this all-powerful God wants to help ordinary people like you and me.

The God of Losers and Failures

As you read the above words of hope and help for people in trouble, you may have been tempted to think, "That's great . . . for some people." You may reason, like many of us do, that God is powerful, available, and willing to help those who are pure, godly, and far more spiritual than you are. But before you jump to that conclusion, note the last line of the stanza. The psalmist adds, "the God of Jacob is [for us] our fortress" (v. 7). Why? Because God knows how some of us think. Our minds tend to work somethng like this: "God, I feel like I'm unworthy of your help. Sure, I could see how you would be a refuge and fortress for those who go to church three times a week, or who are leaders, pastors, and missionaries, but not for someone like me." God included that title for us. When we understand the implications of "God of Jacob," it blows that kind of reasoning out of the water.

The title "God of Jacob" actually indicates who is eligible to receive God's present help in time of trouble. It's a huge relief. It means God will be there for people like Jacob! He's not just God, not just the Lord Almighty, but also, the God of Jacob. Wonder why that's in here? Why the God of Jacob? Why not the God of Abraham or the God of Isaac? Why not at least the God of Israel? (Israel was the new name God gave Jacob after he got his act together.) God's making the point that he's the same God who was there for Jacob, the liar, the loser, the deceiver.

Do you remember who Jacob was? He was one of the first three Hebrew patriarchs. His name means, literally, "the grasper of the

155

heel" or "deceiver." Jacob was the guy who couldn't get it right. Jacob was the guy who was always lying, manipulating, jockeying for position. Jacob was always doing people in. I believe there's a clear message here. It's a message of grace. By calling himself "the God of Jacob" here, God is saying, "I am there for manipulators, and schemers, and people who are living double lives, and hypocrites. I am there for people whose lives aren't together." So, now do you feel eligible? Don't wait to get "good enough" to run to God when you're afraid. Run to him right now and watch how he will not only help you but also change you in the process.

Responding to God

> Come and see the works of the LORD,
>   the desolations he has brought on the earth.
> He makes wars cease to the ends of the earth;
>   he breaks the bow and shatters the spear,
>   he burns the shields with fire.
> "Be still, and know that I am God;
>   I will be exalted among the nations,
>   I will be exalted in the earth."
>
> The LORD Almighty is with us;
>   the God of Jacob is our fortress. *Selah*
>
> verses 8–11

How do you enter in and experience God's presence in times of trouble when you're gripped by fear? There are two commands here; two things we're told to do. Picture yourself and your problem, whatever that is, and then picture God with all his power and resources at your disposal. Now, there are two things you have to do to connect yourself and your problem with God and his resources. Here's the deal:

"Come and see the works of the Lord" (v. 8). You've got to come. In the face of fear, you and I have to move toward God. He implores us; he invites us; he commands us. Help and hope are available, but you've got to come to him.

156

Not only must you come, you must come and see. The word "see" here is very interesting. It not only means to see objectively with your eye, but the same word is used elsewhere in Scripture to refer to a seer or a prophet. It's the idea of looking at life with the inward eye, with spiritual insight. It means you look at the facts but draw back from the facts and say, "What is God doing here? What could God be doing?"

Let's get practical. When you decide to "come and see," what are you to see? The works of the Lord. Now, what did that originally mean to the people reading or hearing this psalm in the day it was written? What were the works of the Lord that they could come and see? What were they to recall in their trouble, when they were surrounded by an army or some life-threatening situation? They would open the Scripture and say, "Now, let's see. The works of the Lord are certainly in Genesis. God created all there is, he promised to preserve us as a people, he promised us a land. Exodus? God delivered the people! Joshua? God delivered the land. First Samuel? God established the kingdom. God chose young David and helped him bring down the giant. They would look at all the battles with the Philistines. They would recount the works of the Lord, his faithfulness in the past.

That's why the psalm says, "The desolations he's brought on the earth" (v. 8). Notice the phrase. The Hebrew people could look back and remember the stories of how God sent the plagues on Egypt, how he devastated their enemies. They could say, "Hey, God's come through for us in the past. The same God is eager to come into my situation right now and be my refuge. Okay."

How can you and I do that? The way we get an accurate view of "the works of the Lord" is from the Scripture, the Bible. But we have to come to the Bible and use our imaginations as we read. That will give you a clear picture of who God is. Seeing what he has done in the past, hearing that the same God is available to you in the present will open your heart to experience his presence.

Now, notice how the tense of the verb changes in the last verses: It goes from what he did in the past to how "he makes wars cease" in the present tense to "I will be exalted in the earth" in the future tense. What are we to come and see? That the same God who did

157

the wondrous works recounted in the Old Testament (past history) has the power to stop wars and conflicts on earth today (present), and the day will come when he has put an end to all conflicts, when he will rule and be exalted over all the earth (eternity future). Come and see who you're dealing with! God Almighty: the same past, present, and future—God eternal. And he's going to take care of all of life. His invitation to you is: You come, look, and remember who God is, what he's done in the past, and what he's going to do in the future. Then you can truly see what he can do for you. If you're still a little fuzzy on how this works out in everyday living in your life and mine, please stay with me. In this next section I'd like to show you how in the midst of your most fearful situations you can learn how to experience God as your refuge and strength.

Experiencing God as Your Refuge and Fortress

How does it specifically happen that you experience God as your refuge? Do you have a rush of warm and giddy feelings that wipe out any sadness, grief, or fear? Do you experience a mystical mist of peace that comes in the room? I mean, how does it work in real life for God to be my strength and my refuge and be available? What does it look like? When fear grips your life, how can you expect to find God and experience his peace?

Before we look at the "how-to" principles of experiencing God as refuge and fortress, I want to introduce you to some people. Their lives illustrate how God does what he promised in Psalm 46. Once you know their stories, you will be able to better grasp the principles that determine your own experience of God's presence in fearful times.

Let's begin with the life of the man who wrote the hymn *A Mighty Fortress Is Our God*. Luther's lyrics certainly show that he understood the concepts. But if you look into his life story and read some of what he wrote during times of great stress and danger, you will see a man who understood and experienced the truth of Psalm 46. God protected him in the way the Bible promised he would.

159

Martin Luther was the great German Bible scholar and reformer. During his lifetime, many who dared to challenge the corrupt religious and political system of the age were burned alive as heretics. Luther boldly read and taught the Scriptures, siding with God's Word rather than religious error. His writings were highly influential, even inflammatory, especially when he dared to post his ninety-five theses on the door of the church in Wittenberg. By publicly challenging and contradicting the corrupt practices of the religious establishment, he brought himself under scrutiny that could have resulted in his execution.

His writings infuriated the emperor, Charles V, who issued a mandate that Luther's writings were to be burned. Rumors began to swirl indicating he was about to be summoned by the authorities. Luther knew full well that he was in imminent danger of execution. But he also knew the God of Psalm 46. We can see his remarkable disposition in a letter he wrote in answer to what he would do if called by the emperor. In a letter dated December 29, 1520, he wrote to Spalatin:

> Of course I would by all means come, if called, in so far as it would be up to me. Even if I could not come by my own power and instead would have to be driven there as a sick man. For if the Emperor summons it would not be right to doubt that I am called by the Lord. Further, if they should employ force in this matter, which is most probable (for they do not want to call me there because they want to learn something), then this matter can only be commended to the Lord. For he who saved the three men in the furnace of the Babylonian king still lives and rules. If he does not want to preserve me, then my head is of slight importance compared with Christ, who was put to death in greatest ignominy—stumbling block to all, and the ruin of many. No one's danger, no one's safety can be considered here. We must rather take care that we do not expose the gospel (which we have finally begun to promote) to the derision of the godless and thus give our enemies a reason for boasting over us because we do not dare confess what we have taught and are afraid to shed our blood for it. May the merciful Christ prevent such cowardice on our part and such boasting on their part. Amen.
>
> . . . Now you have my judgment and my opinion on this matter. You may expect anything of me except flight and recantation.

I do not want to escape, much less recant; may the Lord Jesus strengthen me in this. I could do neither without endangering piety and the salvation of many.

Farewell and be strong in the Lord.[1]

Martin Luther was called before the Diet of Worms, April 17, 1521. The authorities of church and state assembled against him, demanding whether the writings were his, and whether he was ready to recant. When he appeared before them again on April 18, he gave them his shrewd answer, fearlessly. Yes, he had written the works, and he had no intention of recanting. An edict was issued against him. As he was being escorted away by the authorities, a band of his followers (disguised as attackers) rode in on horseback, swooped him off to a German castle—a mighty fortress of sorts—where they hid him and provided all he needed for two years.

Some of his friends heard of the attack and feared the worst. An ambush had been a possible danger. He lived in treacherous times and his outspoken faith pitted him against powerful religious and political forces. An outspoken leader could no longer create problems if he was dead.

However, in the midst of that, God literally provided a mighty fortress, continual provision, joy in the midst of adversity, and calm in the midst of the storm. During those months of seclusion in that castle, Luther translated the New Testament into German. Until this time, Jerome's Latin Bible had been the only approved Bible. Luther's radical confidence in the understandability of God's Word led to his work in putting the Bible into the language of the common people. He placed the Scriptures into the hands of plowboys, schoolgirls, and merchants. Amazing.

Luther's composure was remarkable. His fearlessness, when fear seemed inescapable, confounded his enemies. God provided for him a mighty fortress—making his lyrics personally prophetic. His experience gave evidence of divine protection, internal strength, and a source of overwhelming joy. He knew the God of Jacob as his fortress. Therefore, when it seemed that all the powers of this world came against him, he stood secure and unruffled. Whether he lived or died wasn't the point. He knew God

161

could deliver him, but even if he did not, Luther was safe from fear. God delivered him out of the hands of his enemies.

One word of caution here. It doesn't always work out that God sends a rescue. God was with us when Mom was in the hospital, but she still died. Sometimes, God gives his people fearlessness in the face of grave danger yet doesn't deliver them by helping them escape. Rather, he delivers them through death into his presence in heaven. We see this in the Book of Acts. Stephen was a disciple of Jesus in the early days of the Christian movement. Falsely accused of blasphemy, he was hauled before a religious court. He proved himself a courageous young man and thorough defender of the faith, challenging the corrupt religious leaders of his day. He concluded his comments to them saying, "You stiff-necked people, with uncircumcised hearts and ears! You are just like your fathers: You always resist the Holy Spirit! Was there ever a prophet your fathers did not persecute? They even killed those who predicted the coming of the Righteous One. And now you have betrayed and murdered him—you who have received the law that was put into effect through angels but have not obeyed it" (Acts 7:51–53).

In spite of Stephen's powerful witness, God allowed the intentions of evil men to be carried out. "While they were stoning him, Stephen prayed, 'Lord Jesus, receive my spirit.' Then he fell on his knees and cried out, 'Lord, do not hold this sin against them.' When he had said this, he fell asleep" (Acts 7:59–60).

But you might be thinking, "Okay, well, that's neat to hear how this worked for Martin Luther and someone whose name is in the Bible, but frankly they're way out of my league! Just because you can find some stellar examples out of the annals of history, doesn't exactly show me how this could work for me. Psalm 46: Experiences for Spiritual Superstars, I can buy, but do you really think God still treats people like this today?"

I do. God's protection is not just for spiritual superstars. These were ordinary people who learned to trust and respond to God according to his Word. You may actually be closer to that condition when you're gripped by fear than at any other time. The reason for this is that most of us learn to trust, not because we're noble, brave, or godly, and certainly not because we have it together, but when we don't have any other choice. We are most likely to experience God when we need him desperately. We learn to trust because that's the only option left to us. When we can't escape the fear and it's gripped us by the throat, what choices do we have? Do I face whatever it is on my own, or do I face it with the power and presence of God? For me, I'll take the plan that includes God. I hope you will too. Let me show you how it works so you're prepared the next time fear strikes in your life.

God Is with Ordinary People

Let me show you ordinary people I've seen in our church go through the most terrifying situations with the presence of God in their lives, every bit as real as for Martin Luther and Stephen.

Will South

I was called to the ICU to visit a fellow named Will South before he went in for quintuple bypass surgery. His arteries were not only plugged, they had dried out and deteriorated to the point that the doctors had to replace major sections. They explained it all to Will and asked, "Do you still want to go through with the surgery?"

He said, "Well, sure."

They said, "You need to understand that the chances of success for this surgery are smaller than for a total heart transplant."

He said, "Well, sure. The options are, if I die, great. I know where I'm going. I've had seven strokes. I'm ready. I believe God wants me to do it."

Knowing all of that, I went to meet with Will early that morning. Will has been a dear friend. Every Saturday night, no matter how he feels, he and I and another man go into a closet and pray together before the services. Every day Will prays for me. He prays for all of our pastors and all their kids by name, every day. During his hospitalizations he'd say, "God gave me the ministry of intercession when he put me flat on my back." He said, "These have been the most delightful years of my life." Will's attitude was remarkable; he was fearless and totally confident in God.

I didn't want to lose Will. But, I confess I went in thinking that this was probably my last time to see Will this side of heaven. Medically speaking, I realized that unless God did a big thing here, this might be it. So, I was uptight, but I wanted to encourage Will and his wife, Sarah. Again, I was asking God, "What do I say?" Again, I read Psalm 46. We talked about the psalm for two or three minutes, then Will started asking about my son, "Hey, how's Ryan? Boy, I just love that kid. What instrument did he play this week on the worship team? You know, when I was a kid . . ." Then he started telling me about how he had chances to lead people to Christ when he was a kid, and he talked about music. Then he asked about my daughter, "Annie, sure is growing." He was totally focused on my family, "Hey, how's your wife? You know, Chip, you shouldn't be here. Your schedule is so busy."

I was astounded at his composure. I was thinking, "Will! I'm supposed to be here to encourage you, not the other way around." It was obvious that the Lord was "for him a refuge." Will broke into a big smile and said, "Isn't God good!" I don't mean in a phony way. He was living the real deal. He was just expressing what an honor it was to be in the presence of the living God, especially in such a time of trouble. He was living proof that "a river makes glad the city of God."

I said, "Yeah, Will. God is good."

He said, "I am so hungry. I want some eggs over medium. They said I can't have any tonight, but I told them tomorrow, after I get out of this Intensive Care, man, I want some eggs over medium. Well, hey, Chip, you've got a lot to get going on. I will see you later. Why don't we pray?" So we prayed.

I came home that night and told my wife, Theresa, "Honey, I spent time with someone today who not only knows God like few people I know but really understands the reality of heaven and eternal perspective." God's presence gave Will gladness in the midst of trouble. It was a privilege to see that firsthand. Will got through that surgery; six months later he was back at church helping out, praying, still asking about my kids and caring about how we were doing.

John Biggs and His Loved Ones

God being your refuge, your fortress, your strength, doesn't mean it always turns out the way you want. It means he's enough, regardless of how it turns out, even when the situation turns out the way you prayed it wouldn't. Let me take you back to the story of John Biggs, the young man I introduced earlier in this chapter who was diagnosed with cancer. John battled cancer for two and a half years, but in the end he died. He died before he got married, before the dreams his parents had for him could be fulfilled. Was God there for Carl and Phyllis Biggs and for John's fiancée, Christine? Was God there for John? You bet. Phyllis and Carl Biggs, along with Christine, shared their reflections with our church family after John passed away. Their words, composed in wrenching grief, rang with authentic experiences of God's presence.

John's Mom: "That first day, we still didn't know what form of cancer John had or anything about it. We just knew it was cancer. That much was very, very frightening. I was so terrified and confused. I had no idea how to handle this. Nothing had ever prepared me to hear something like that about my child. It would have been easier to hear it about myself. I wrestled with it all evening. And then I went home and wrestled again all night. I just kept thinking, 'I just want to run away and hide. Where can I go? I've got to get away from this.'

"Finally, about 4:30 in the morning, all that kept coming back to me was the first verse of Psalm 46, that God is our refuge. That word 'refuge' just kept jumping out at me. I finally gave up the struggle to figure it out. I reached the point of surrender where I said, *'Lord, I can't do this. I don't know how to do this. So I'm just going to choose to trust you and let you be my refuge.'* Amazingly, I actually slept for the next two hours.

"God led me through Psalm 46, over and over again. I read it many times a day for the two and a half years of John's illness. I clung to those verses for dear life. And bit by bit, that description of God became such a reality to me. God was the strength that got me out of bed every morning to put one foot in front of the other. He's the one who did everything. One version I read trans-

165

lated ever-present as 'very present.' He was so close; so very, very present. God was very, very real to us and a very present help—and that certainly was a time of trouble.

"There's a song called 'Trust His Heart.' It describes many of the situations in life that are beyond our understanding. The one phrase I clung to from that song was, *'when you can't see his hand, trust his heart.'* We may not know what or how, but we always know God's why—because he loves. We can trust that truth. That's what we had to do with John and that terrible disease. There was nothing else to trust and no one else to run to. As time went on and things got worse—and we knew from the first week that it was not going to be curable—we experienced God's presence in ways and at times that can only be described as supernaturally comforting. The doctors were giving our son only months to live. God helped him fool them all by living for two and a half years, but all that time we lived with the immediate threat of death. We got very familiar with the valley of the shadow of death. But I kept going back to Psalm 46, trusting God to show me, to make some sense of it, and to get us through it; and he has.

"God has been so, so present. That part is the best part of all. There were times when I was awake at three o'clock in the morning, crying out in despair, not knowing what to do . . . I couldn't sleep. I couldn't be awake. I couldn't do anything; but when I cried out to God, I would feel this incredible warmth wrap around me. Physically, I felt his arms around me. He and I were the only two in that room. I would feel arms around me and I knew it was God. He was right there. He really carried us through it.

John's Dad: "When I got the call at the office that the results had come back and John had cancer, I thought, 'This isn't real. This happens to other people, not to our family.' This happened during a period when things were going great for our family. We thought we were invincible. And then this hit. As a father, you know how it is, you have great love and aspirations for what your son is going to do. We had to come to real grips with the fact that God had a different plan. And how did God reveal it? He actually revealed it through John. John taught us all so much about trust and about totally leaning on God.

166

"We went through the whole denial thing. You know, thinking it's like he's got the flu. It's going to get better. It's fixable. God's going to take care of it. But, last summer it became evident that God was going to choose to heal John in a much different way than we were all praying he would. He was going to heal him by taking him home to be with him. Even through that realization the last couple of months, John was determined to praise God. He was here in church, in a wheelchair, even the day before he died. God was present with him; there was no denying it for any of us close to him. And you know what God taught us, what God taught me through my son? That he was there; that God is here. God is ever-present, and he will take care of us and will look after us—no matter what the circumstance."

Christine, John's fiancée: "I think this has been the best year of my life, getting engaged. John and I had all these dreams and plans. I had a lot of faith, praying and believing that God would heal him. I still believe God can do anything. I knew that. Even at this point, I don't feel disappointed. God healed him in a different way.

"I was so caught up in planning our life together, and our dreams, and all these things. Something that really touched me was when they looked me in the eyes and said, "It's going to be really soon." Then, all of a sudden, it was like a whirlwind. I was thinking, 'Okay, this is not going to happen. Things are going to be different.' That's the point when I had to stop and be still. I had to stop and completely surrender myself to God, and say to myself, 'Okay, I have all these ideas, and all these plans, and all these dreams, but the fact is that God is in control. God knows the plans for our lives and he knows what is best.'

"John was the one who taught me that we need to live for today. I was living in the future and our dreams. Then there was this transitional thought, 'Now! I've got to live for today.' The last couple of months I tried to focus on that and spend the time we had together well. It was really cool because God brought so much joy into that time. It was probably the most difficult time, but all the while—because we were living for each day, moment by moment literally, not knowing what was going to happen from day to day—there was so much joy and such rich times together. So, God was definitely there.

167

"Now, I think of him more as my fortress, a place of rest where I can go to reflect. It all happened so fast, but God is still my fortress where I can retreat to be still and ask things like, 'How can I learn from this loss? How can I grow from this experience? How can I go on? And, how can I help other people?'"

Christine's comments lead us to the second command God gives us in order to fully experience the promise of his presence given us in Psalm 46. It is: "**Be still, and know that I am God.** I will be exalted among the nations. I will be exalted in the earth." And then the refrain, "The Lord Almighty is with us." Or, literally, he is for us. Not only are we to come and see the works of the Lord. We are to be still and know that he is God. This passage is often used as a nice devotional sentiment. Meditation is great. Getting quiet before the Lord is wonderful. But that is not what this passage is teaching.

Literally, "Be still" means cease striving. Stop! Knock it off! Get your hands off the deal! Hold off! Surrender! Unfortunately, God has to be blunt with us. Why? Because when we're in trouble, our tendency is to try to do something—anything. We get afraid and we get moving—often in the wrong direction. We jockey for position, we manipulate, and we try to cut deals with God. You know, "God, I'll do this if you'll do that." We get frantic. God gently says, "When you're in real trouble, I'll tell you what. You will meet me on my terms. Be still." It's the same kind of phrase Jesus used when he was in the boat with the disciples in the storm. They screamed, "Don't you care that we're perishing, Lord? What are you going to do?" And he said, "Peace! Be still." Instantly, the winds and the waves ceased all movement. That's the idea. Just stop and know that he's God. You're not.

Why can we be still in frightful times? Because God will be exalted. This is a picture to remind us that the future is sure; God knows how all the battles will end, and he's going to be the ultimate victor—and he's on your side. It makes sense to stop and surrender your fear to him. Practically, this takes the form of a prayer of absolute surrender and dependency. You take all the chips of your life, all the cards, and all the strategies, and you push them all to the middle of the table and let God take it from there. It's yours, God. I give. You call the shots. I need you and I'm in.

This is what it means to be still. And when you do that, the Lord Almighty will be with you. The God of grace, the God of Jacob, will be for you a refuge.

Trusting God in All Circumstances

Now, I hope you're saying, "Chip, are you really telling me that in the midst of great adversity, I mean pressure and trouble and fear, that God's presence could actually give me joy?"

Yes.

"You want me to believe that God could actually get me out of danger?"

Yes.

"You're telling me that the worst thing I could imagine could happen and God's presence would get me through it with external protection, internal strength, and a constant stream of joy in the midst of adversity?"

Yes.

The next time you are gripped by fear, let Psalm 46 fill you with hope and confidence. That confidence can be yours before you know how it's going to turn out. Martin Luther wrote, "He who saved the three men in the furnace of the Babylonian king still lives and rules." He was referring to the events recorded in the Book of Daniel when three Hebrew exiles, renamed Shadrach, Meshach, and Abednego, were commanded to bow before an idol or be burned alive in a fiery furnace. They didn't know how it was going to turn out, but they chose to face their worst fears with confidence in God.

You see, sometimes it may get worse before it gets better. But the hope and confidence of Psalm 46 is what happens before you even know how it's going to turn out. You can have the same kind of confidence these three Hebrew teens had. They said, "We know God can rescue us out of danger, but even if he doesn't we're going to trust and obey him." What happened? They were cast into the furnace alive. And guess who was there with them in the flames? The same God who will be your "ever-present help [in your times of] trouble."

LIFE LESSONS TO APPLY

1. Remember that God is for us: a refuge, strength, and ever-present help in times of trouble.

   Action Step: *Run to him in prayer the moment you begin to fear.*

2. Come and see the works of the Lord.

   Action Step: *Stop and reflect on God's past deliverances and answers to prayer in your life and in the pages Scripture.*

3. Be still! Cease striving and know that he is God Almighty, and he is with you in your frightful situation.

   Action Step: *Surrender your expectations to God and stop trying to work out all the circumstances in your own power and strength.*

4. Trust God to give you sustenance and joy, even in the midst of terrifying circumstances.

   Action Step: *Memorize Psalm 46:1–3 and quote it every time fear grips your heart.*

EXPERIENCING GOD WHEN YOU ARE GRIPPED BY FEAR

Somewhere you can turn: Psalm 46

KEY VERSES

God is our refuge and strength,
an ever-present help in trouble.
Therefore we will not fear, though the earth give way
and the mountains fall into the heart of the sea.
The Lord Almighty is with us;
the God of Jacob is our fortress.

Psalm 46:1–2, 7

6

I am with you . . .

WHEN YOU'VE BLOWN IT BIG TIME

Sometimes smart people do dumb things. Sometimes wise people do foolish things. Sometimes godly people do sinful things. And when we blow it big time, we need God's help, more than perhaps at any other time.

In the days surrounding the Super Bowl in 1999, a player named Eugene Robinson made national news. This guy is smart. He is not just well educated; he is sharp on the playing field of life. He has made a career in the NFL by intercepting passes. When quarterbacks throw the ball, he figures out where it will go and then steals it. In football he is a team leader, and because of his spotless Christian testimony, he is an inspirational leader. He has a great track record as a competitor and as a godly role model.

Right after the Super Bowl, I had a meeting scheduled with two men from a publishing house preparing to release a book by Eugene Robinson. He seemed to be center stage. On the Saturday before the Super Bowl, Athletes in Action, a Christian ministry, gave Eugene their Outstanding Citizen Award for demonstrating the godliest character in the NFL that year. He was viewed as one of the most consistent Christians in professional sports. He spent Saturday giving interviews to the media. During them, he made a public witness of his relationship with Jesus Christ.

That night Eugene Robinson did a dumb, foolish, and sinful thing. This all-star, Christian leader and role model had a confrontation with a pair of handcuffs. An undercover female cop arrested Eugene for soliciting prostitution. He landed in jail. His wife's phone rang in the middle of the night. His coaches were called. The news got out. Suddenly, the reporters who had interviewed him the day before had a surprise ending for their stories.

But for those who loved Eugene and looked up to him, it was a terrible twist.

We read this, shake our heads, and say, "How? Why? What was behind that?" You should have seen those two men from the publishing company. They weren't excited about the ten thousand fliers they had sent to Miami to publicize Eugene's book. Instead they were wondering, "What in the world do we do with this book now?"

But Eugene Robinson was left wondering something more profound. Would God help him now that he had blown it big time? His life had seemed like a sure touchdown pass. Would he be intercepted and run back to score for the opposition? Would God turn his back on Eugene after this moral fumble?

Before you shake your head at him, wait up. He's not the first smart person to do a dumb thing. He's not the first godly person to do a sinful thing, and he won't be the last. People who love God with all their hearts—including the person writing this book—have done foolish and utterly sinful things. I am going to guess—just take a wild stab—that every person who reads this book has done a few dumb, unwise, and sinful things too. Our private sins may not make the headlines, but that doesn't make them okay.

You may have done things that you hope no one ever finds out about. You may be hiding something desperately shameful in your past. No one knows about that abortion. No one knows that you encouraged the abortion. No one knows about that brief fling, the shady business deal, the things you stole, the secret late nights in front of the computer screen, the adult theaters you visited, or the impure thought life that threatens to be played out. No one knows about the scheming, the lying, or the cheating we have all done in our past or even struggle with in the present. Your cover isn't blown. You haven't been caught yet. But you know, and God knows.

Another Man Who Blew It Big Time

Here is a true story about a godly man who blew it big time by anybody's yardstick. He was a king of Israel and his name was David. He was smart, wise, and as godly as they come; but he was at the wrong place at the wrong time. He was a good man at a weak moment, basically channel surfing on his palace roof during a hot spring night. He saw a woman named Bathsheba bathing. Just like pornography draws people in today, he was drawn in. He saw, he looked, and then he kept looking. He sent for her and committed adultery with her, even though her husband was one of his loyal soldiers away on a military mission. A while later, Bathsheba sent the king a message, "I'm pregnant." David tried to cover his sin by getting her husband, Uriah, to come off the battlefield and sleep with her. That way he would think the baby was his own. Hey, who would have to know? That plan didn't work. David hadn't counted on Uriah's honor and sense of duty. So David had Bathsheba's husband killed in battle and covered up the murder as a casualty of war.

No One Gets Away with It

Several months later, God sent a prophet named Nathan to confront David. Nathan gave him God's message in a little story because confronting kings directly in that day was a good way to lose your head. Here is the story Nathan told King David:

> There were two men in a certain town, one rich and the other poor. The rich man had a large number of sheep and cattle, but the poor man had nothing except one little ewe lamb that he had bought. He raised it, and it grew up with him and his children. It shared his food, drank from his cup and even slept in his arms. It was like a daughter to him.
>
> Now a traveler came to the rich man, but the rich man refrained from taking one of his own sheep or cattle to prepare a meal for the traveler who had come to him. [Hospitality was highly valued in that culture. When a guest arrived, the host was obliged to provide a meal. This was understood.] Instead, he took the ewe lamb that belonged to the poor man and prepared it for the one who had come to him.
>
> 2 Samuel 12:1b–4

Now bear in mind that Nathan knew King David had grown up as a shepherd. David understood about sheep and getting attached to them. David erupted in anger against the rich man in the story and said to Nathan, "As surely as the LORD lives the man who did this deserves to die! He must pay for that lamb four times over because he did such a thing and had no pity!" (2 Sam. 12:5–6). Can you imagine the veins bulging out of David's neck? Can you feel his indignation? Can you see the wheels turning in his mind as he rages? How could anyone do such a thing? He was hot! And his reaction was right. He just didn't realize his indignation should have been addressed toward himself.

When the Finger Points at You

The account in Scripture captures the tension and drama of the moment: "Then Nathan said to David, 'You are the man! This is what the LORD, the God of Israel, says, "I anointed you king over Israel and I delivered you from the hand of Saul. I gave your master's house to you and your master's wives in your arms. I gave you the house of Israel and Judah. And if all of this had been too little, I would have given you even more. Why did you despise the word of the LORD by doing what is evil in his eyes? You struck down Uriah the Hittite with the sword and took his wife to be your own. You killed him with the sword of the Ammonites. Now therefore . . .'"' (2 Sam. 12:7–10a). Watch out. Here comes the discipline.

Nathan continued, "'The sword will never depart from your house, because you despised me and took the wife of Uriah the Hittite to be your own.' This is what the Lord says. 'Out of your own household I'm going to bring calamity upon you. Before your very eyes I will take your wives and give them to one who is close to you, and he will lie with your wives in broad daylight. You did it in secret, but I will do this thing in broad daylight before all Israel'" (2 Sam. 12:10b–12).

Nathan's story took four verses. God's verdict through Nathan took six verses. Confrontation led to scathing condemnation followed immediately by crushing consequences. There was no way

178

of escape for the king. Finally, Nathan took a breath. David could have easily made it his last.

Then something quite amazing happened in the throne room. A king did what kings weren't supposed to do. "David said to Nathan, 'I have sinned against the Lord'" (2 Sam. 12:13a). David added no excuses, didn't shift the blame to others, he simply acknowledged his sin.

"Nathan replied, 'The Lord has taken away your sin. You are not going to die'" (2 Sam. 12:13b). Under the law the penalty for adultery or murder was death. David knew that, but Nathan decreed God's pardon. Nathan continued, "But because by doing this you have made the enemies of the Lord show utter contempt, the son born to you will die" (2 Sam. 12:14). When David realized he had blown it big time, he cried out to God. God answered with truth and discipline, but also with a pardon.

Failure Never Has to Be Final with God

One thing all human beings have in common is failure. David failed big time, but that wasn't the end of it. It was a moment when all could have been lost; but it wasn't. With God failure never has to be final! No matter how bad, how wrong, how ashamed, how embarrassed you may rightly feel, God is there for you. Even though you knew better, you knew it was a dumb move, and you knew it was unwise—God is willing to meet you. He may even send a Nathan to let you know he knows everything. At times like these we need to turn to God like David did. Will there be consequences? Sure. Will there be pain? Of course. Does it have to ruin your life forever? No, absolutely not.

Failure Raises Pressing Questions

✓ How can you ever recover when you know you've done something terribly wrong?
✓ How do you erase the guilt, shame, and embarrassment?

✓ How do you find courage and strength to deal with all the consequences?

✓ How do you restore your relationship with God?

✓ Can you restore relationships with the people you have hurt?

✓ Can you return to a good life after doing something you knew was wrong in your heart of hearts but did anyway?

✓ Can you ever recover from the huge fallout you know would rightfully come if the truth were known?

Don't worry, I am not going to give you pat answers to all these questions. Easy answers to such serious questions deserve to get brushed off. There are no simple formulas to solve such problems. When you and I face these kinds of real questions, we know—deep down—we need more than a theoretical answer. We certainly need more than a line we can use on God. We need a gracious, merciful, and loving God to show up and do something to make a difference.

Can You Relate?

When I shared this message with the people in our church, you should have seen the body language of the congregation. It revealed that plenty of them could relate to Eugene Robinson and King David. They were thinking, "I have been there!" or "I am there right now." I can't see your body language, so I don't know, but you may have some stuff in your past or some things that are stinging your conscience right now. You may be thinking, "He's got my number. Boy, if there is any way, I want to get back to God. I don't think I can. I may have messed up too badly. I feel dirty. I feel ashamed. I feel unworthy."

No matter how you feel or what you have done, God is willing to show up to help you. One of the ways he will do it is through the words of that man David who failed so miserably! God is with you—always . . . even when you blow it big time.

PSALM 51

Psalm 51 is a rare piece of literature. David wrote out his personal, private prayer after Nathan, the prophet, confronted David with his sin. It's the prayer of a wise and godly king who lost his way but was found by a loving, righteous God. It's the prayer of an adulterer, liar, schemer, betrayer, and murderer caught in the act. Please don't think God showed up for David just because he was a king of Israel. God had deposed kings throughout their history. David had no protected position. Nathan's verbal flurry pummeled the king into the corner. What set David apart was his contrite response and sincere heart toward God and others when he realized he'd blown it. Looking at how God showed up for David can teach us to align our hearts rightly with God, so he will show up for us too and provide a remedy for our sins.

Seven Steps, a Challenge, and a Promise

As you carefully read Psalm 51, you will discover seven clearly definable steps to spiritual recovery in this prayer. I warn you up front, however, using these steps will take great spiritual integrity and courage. But if you are willing to respond God's way, the God of the universe will be there for you.

Remember these seven steps are not the solution to your problems—*God* is the solution. However, they will put you in a spiritual disposition to experience God working in your life in a real way that will make a difference when you've blown it. They do not constitute a formula for forgiveness and restoration but define a process that must occur in our hearts as we deal with the guilt, shame, and consequences of our sin. Apart from God, following these steps will do nothing more than disillusion you. He put this prayer in the Bible, so we could hear David's heart crying out to God and learn from him. Let's do it.

STEP 1: Come Clean

The first step is to come clean with God. Get honest. Get it out in the open. Stop trying to rationalize, minimize, excuse, and spin. Break out of denial. David was in denial for a long time; finally, Nathan told him a story and the truth broke through. His response was, "I have sinned against the LORD."

> Have mercy on me, O God,
>   according to your unfailing love;
> according to your great compassion
>   blot out my transgressions.
> Wash away all my iniquity
>   and cleanse me from my sin.
>
> For I know my transgressions,
>   and my sin is always before me.
> Against you, you only, have I sinned
>   and done what is evil in your sight,
> so that you are proved right when you speak
>   and justified when you judge.
>
>   verses 1–4

Notice the progression here. You don't get to step 2 unless you do step 1. You have to stop and say, "I've blown it, Lord, and here's how I've blown it." David had to be honest. He came clean with God, with himself, and with those close to him. God brought him to that turning point in his life. While flying from Dallas to San Jose recently, I read a book from New Life Clinics that addressed why this first step is often the hardest. The author noted three reasons people won't come clean.[1]

1. Fear of Losing Our Reputation

The fear of being publicly exposed can keep us awake at night with feelings of dread. Revealing our failures and admitting that we've fallen short of perfection to even one person might result in rejection. This is a valid reason for fear, but it is not a valid reason to avoid confession. It is still better to be found out, even to have a damaged reputation, than to allow venomous secrets to poison our relationship with God and others. We can counteract this fear by getting to know God better. When we are convinced that God is who he says he is—forgiving, protecting, able to deliver, and eager to restore—fear will diminish because we will trust him to respond according to his character.

2. Fear of Losing Our Favorite Sin

Another reason we recoil from confession is that it requires us to renounce unhealthy habits. Those of us who seek God must leave behind everything that detracts from or works against God's purpose for our lives. When we confess sinful attitudes, behaviors, or relationships, we must also take steps to abandon them. Until we renounce the sin, we haven't repented.

3. Fear of Losing Our Security

When our emotional or financial security is linked to something sinful, naturally we will fear confession. Confession will bring change, and the immediate change may not seem good. This is where faith comes in. If we agree with God about what he says is good, we can trust that the ultimate outcome of obedience will be good as well.

When You Don't Come Clean

There is an alternative to confession; it's called pain. Before Nathan confronted him, David wrote, "Blessed is the man whose sin the LORD does not count against him and in whose spirit is no deceit. When I kept silent, my bones wasted away through my groaning all day long. For day and night your hand was heavy upon me; my strength was sapped as in the heat of summer" (Ps. 32:2–4).

David described a weight that kept growing in his soul until it was crushing him. He was saying, "I was like a desert. I was like a parched land. I was depressed. I was torn up." You can choose not to come clean, but if you don't, the weight of guilt, of a dirty conscience, of secrecy will eventually crush you. It will dry you up emotionally. It will dry you up physically and spiritually. The final price tag of covering up our sin is far greater than the price, no matter how big you fear it might be, of coming clean.

On What Basis Can We Ask for Mercy?

David's prayer begins with a request for mercy. He asks this on the basis of God's character of unfailing love and great compassion. That was the reason he could ask God, "Blot out my transgressions" (v. 1b). The reason we can dare to come clean with God is because we too can trust his character, which has not changed. God does not accept our confession based on our spotless character or our good deeds. Nothing in us can counteract the bad. At the moment of our confession, our future rests entirely on God's unfailing love and great compassion.

Let's look at these two aspects of God's character more closely:

Unfailing Love: a Hebrew word that means a loyal covenant love. This is the love God demonstrated through the covenants he made with people. This is God's I'll-keep-my-end-of-our-relationship kind of love. These covenants are given to us in the Bible. The Old Testament introduced and illustrated God's promise to cover and atone for sin. God accepted animal sacrifices and the blood of animals offered by faith according to the clearly prescribed rituals he laid out in the Old Testament law. Today we have absolute confidence in God's unfailing love based on Christ's blood offered as a sacrifice for our sins once and for all.

Compassion: The word's original meaning made reference to "the womb," or "internal organs," where Hebrews believed the seat of our emotions dwelt. Compassion is that aspect of God's character that wells up in him as pity and concern at the sight of our deepest needs and hurts. It calls on the depths of God's almighty love, the love that goes far deeper than we can fathom.

David dared to come clean with God because he shamelessly relied on God's unfailing love and compassion. If you don't know that aspect of God's nature, you will probably be afraid to risk taking the first step. If you're too scared to come clean, maybe you don't know that God's love and compassion never fails. Jesus' death on the cross reminds us that God is not surprised by our sin but has in fact made provision for fallen people like you and me to receive forgiveness and compassion when we fail.

No Trying to Cut a Deal

David didn't try to cut a deal or negotiate a settlement. He didn't say, "If you will let the boy live, then I will . . ."—no way. When you're guilty, like David knew he was, you've got to come clean before God without any conditions.

STEP 2: Ask God's Forgiveness

Look carefully at the italicized verbs David used for his four requests: "*Have mercy* on me, O God, according to your unfailing love; according to your great compassion *blot out* my transgressions. *Wash away* all my iniquity and *cleanse* me from my sin" (vv. 1–2).

He clearly asked God to forgive him and to remove his sins. "Mercy" applies to God's willingness; "blot out," "wash away," and "cleanse" apply to God's work in our lives, cleaning up the mess we have created. We need to be that clear when we have

185

blown it. No hedging about whether or not we've done anything wrong. Then we must ask God to forgive us of the specific sins we have committed.

STEP 3: Accept Responsibility for Your Sin

Count the times in these verses that David owned his own sin. You do not hear a victim's mentality. You do not hear him say, "The devil made me do it," or "I was just having a bad day." You do not hear blame shifting like "I don't know who the guard was—he never should have let that lady in the door," or "That general of mine! He knew that was a bad command. He should never have let Uriah be killed like that."

Notice the five different times in the next three verses where David specifically and personally claimed responsibility for his sin: "Wash away all *my iniquity* and cleanse me from *my sin*. For I know *my transgressions*, and *my sin* is always before me. Against you, you only, *have I sinned* and done what is evil in your sight, so that you are proved right when you speak and justified when you judge" (vv. 2–4).

Five times in three verses David took responsibility for his own sin. And—in case you are wondering—he never blamed his mother. He did not mean anything inherently sinful happened in his conception. He was admitting, "I have a sin problem that goes beyond just a bad choice with Bathsheba and a wrong decision about her husband." He did not blame anyone but himself. Every alcoholic, drug addict, sex addict, gossip, backbiter, or liar who made it out of that pattern of sin had to take responsibility for his or her actions. Each had to stop blaming others.

> Surely I was sinful at birth,
>   sinful from the time my mother conceived me.
>
> verse 5

186

Notice how David owned responsibility for his sin, while acknowledging that the real issue went back to the moment he was conceived. He saw sin as a problem in the core of his being, not just a symptom. His insight rings true. All humanity has an inborn sin nature. We're all prone to do what we know is wrong, even while there's a part of us that hates wrong and really wants to do right. However, David didn't use the recognition that he was born with this bent toward sin as an excuse or justification for his sinful actions as many in our culture do.

Hey, I Deserve Whatever I Get!

David not only owned the sin but also the consequences. He'd already heard Nathan, hadn't he? "The sword will never depart from your house. Someone close to you is going to sleep with your wives in broad daylight. The baby boy Bathsheba just delivered is going to die." He knew there was going to be severe judgment; but notice how he said to God, "You are justified when you judge." It's like saying, "Hey, I deserve whatever I get." When you take that attitude toward God, he will be inclined to respond to you.

We understand this. Have you ever been betrayed deeply? There's only one thing worse than being betrayed, isn't there? It's when people lie about what they have done afterwards, trying to wiggle out of their responsibility. I don't know about you, but I am more compassionate when my kids come to me and say, "Dad, I blew it. I'm sorry, it was wrong. Hey, if I'm grounded for the next ninety-five years, okay. I deserve whatever I get."

But if my kids tell me part of the truth and cover up some important details, they are setting the stage for trouble. When I discover more facts and they have to reveal another little part of the story, my temperature goes up. As a dad, it makes me angry not to be trusted with the truth, even when it's ugly. What do you do as a parent when you are lied to? How do you feel when you're not trusted? Doesn't it make you angry? Absolutely. Do you know why? It's because you are made in the image of God. That's how God feels when we don't accept full responsibility for our own sins and accept whatever consequences he allows.

187

God Is a Loving Disciplinarian

God is not like the parent who gives the spanking and then leaves you alone to think about what you have done. He is more like the parent who lovingly administers the discipline then takes you in his arms and comforts you. He may indeed mete out punishment, but he cries when you cry and stays with you to help you bear it. Some of the most precious experiences of God's presence in your life can be when God draws near to give you the grace to bear the consequences of your sin.

STEP 4: Accept God's Forgiveness on God's Terms

As a pastor, I frequently see people trying to cut deals with God. It sounds something like this. First, they carry on an internal monologue, "If I come clean, I could lose my job. I may lose my family. If I come clean, boy, what will people think of me?" Then they say to God, "I tell you what I will do, God. I'll start going to church more regularly, be a better husband, be a better man, give money to missions . . . If you let me keep this secret and not let anyone find out, I'll never do anything like this again. In fact, I'll be . . ."

If you tend to think this way, let me help you out. You can't cut deals with God. You're not dealing with some small self-made god you can hide things from. You've got to come to God on his terms. He provides a way for you to be forgiven, but it's not by trading in a few good deeds or promising to make up for what you've done.

> Surely you desire truth in the inner parts;
> you teach me wisdom in the inmost place.
>
> verse 6

David recognized that a prerequisite to receiving forgiveness was honestly facing what he had done wrong. He recognized that the basis for a real relationship with God is honesty. God wants it from the heart, from our innermost parts.

As David reflects on God's desires, he makes a shift. In the original language, this is clearer. You can see how he used the future tense. Literally he was saying, "You *will* teach me wisdom in the inmost place." This wisdom he had in mind refers to an intellectual understanding and skill in living the right way.

What Cleans Up Sin?

> Cleanse me with hyssop, and I will be clean;
>   wash me, and I will be whiter than snow.
> Let me hear joy and gladness;
>   let the bones you have crushed rejoice.
> Hide your face from my sins
>   and blot out all my iniquity.
>
> verses 7–9

Hyssop was a little herb the Jews would dip in blood for use in ritual cleansing. David's phrase pictures God performing a ceremonial cleansing. In the Old Testament God made it clear that there was no forgiveness of sins without the shedding of blood. The people had to put their faith in God that he would accept the blood of animals as promised in the covenant. David was declaring his belief that God will do what he has promised. He was literally saying, "You will wash me and I will be whiter than snow. You will let me hear joy and gladness." He accepted that God's mode of cleansing was sufficient because God was doing the cleanup. Then he declared it.

"Yeah, But I Can't Forgive Myself"

It's one thing to ask God to forgive and cleanse you; but to complete the process you must accept it. Unfortunately, that's not what I hear when people pour out their hearts to me. This is especially true when people have done something that deeply violates their conscience. Maybe they had an affair. Maybe they really hurt someone. Maybe they've done something totally out of character. They say, "Yeah, it's all in my past. It was many years ago. I know intellectually that God's forgiven me, but . . . " You probably already know what they say. "I know God forgives me, *but I can't forgive myself.*" Have you heard that?

In my early years as a Christian, when I blew it, I would experience overwhelming guilt. I remember feeling like a failure and promising God I would never do it again. Then I kept doing it, again and again. I'd stop myself and say, "Okay, I know the Scripture says Christ died for me and all my sins, past, present, and future. I know it says that when I confess my sin, he is faithful and just to forgive my sins and cleanse me from all unrighteousness." But I also used to say, "I can't forgive myself." I would be depressed over small sins for a day or two and big sins for a week or two. Then I would gradually let myself off the hook because I felt I had suffered enough or because I was now dealing with a new reason for guilt!

That's theologically inaccurate and spiritually deadly. It produced a vicious cycle of sin, guilt, shame, depression, and distance from God. Finally, I had someone sit me down, open a Bible, and show me how arrogant and unbelieving I was in doing that. By saying I needed to forgive myself after God had already provided forgiveness for my sins on his terms, I was putting a little spin on things to make me the center of my universe. What audacity for me to put my chest out and say, "The fact that I can't forgive myself means more than God's forgiveness!"

I don't mean to sound harsh, but you and I are not that important. You may not feel good about yourself for a long time. You may never—and perhaps should never—feel good when you think about what you did wrong and how that impacted others; but your forgiveness is not based on your emotions. Your emotions can and will lie to you. It doesn't matter how badly you sinned or how badly you feel about it. What it was, when it was, or how it was done, does nothing to change this truth: If you ask for forgiveness from God on the basis of his unfailing covenant love, *you are forgiven*. Accept it.

David's acceptance of God's forgiveness gives us great confidence. He committed murder. I hope you don't have that one hanging over you, at least not in the literal sense, but even if you do, God can forgive you (although forgiveness from God doesn't mean you escape the consequences). We've all murdered with our mouths. God can forgive that too. David committed adultery, not just by lusting in his imagination, but in the flesh. God forgave him. He betrayed his family, his nation, one of his most dedicated soldiers, and God. Still, he had the confidence to say, "You will teach me wisdom. You will purge me. You will cleanse me. You will restore to me my joy." He wasn't saying he deserved that. He was declaring the goodness and mercy and faithfulness of God. We too need to accept God's forgiveness, according to his covenant given to us in the Bible, then declare that God has done it.

STEP 5: Request a Fresh Work of God's Grace

When you've blown it big time you need a fresh work of God's grace. And you need to request it. It doesn't come automatically. Look at how David did this.

> Create in me a pure heart, O God,
>   and renew a steadfast spirit within me.
> Do not cast me from your presence
>   or take your Holy Spirit from me.
>
> verses 10–11

The word "create" is an amazing word. It's the same word used in Genesis when God created something out of nothing. Think! When God speaks, he has the power to bring something into existence—from nothing! David recognized that he was asking for nothing less than a miracle. He was saying, "God, I'm asking you to miraculously create a pure heart in this dirty, defiled man that I am."

Then he said, *"Renew a steadfast spirit within me."* You know why? What do you want to do when you've sinned badly? If you're like me, you want to run away from God, run from peo-

191

ple, and give up. So what was he praying? He was asking God to give him the spirit he needed to hang in there, to face whatever would come without running. When God shows up, he can do a fresh work of grace in your spirit that will keep you from running.

When David said, "Do not cast me from your presence or take your Holy Spirit from me," he may well have been thinking about what happened to King Saul. He'd seen it with his own eyes. He lived in a time when the Spirit of God came on people on occasion. The Spirit didn't dwell in them. When God was done using a person, or sometimes when a person sinned, God took the Spirit away. That's what happened to Saul. So David said, "Oh, God, please don't remove your Holy Spirit."

> Restore to me the joy of your salvation
> and grant me a willing spirit, to sustain me.
>
> verse 12

This leads us to David's final plea. When we've blown it and we know it, when we lose the joy of our salvation, we should cry out to God like David did. It was his way of saying, "God, I want the intimacy I once had with you back again. I want to go into worship again and feel free. I want to have the sense that when I pray, you are there. When I read your Word, I long to have it jump off the page as you speak to me. I want that sense of your presence. I want that fellowship we used to have before I sinned and before I started playing games. I want to experience your arms, your heart, and your approval; I want it back."

When David got to the point where he said, "Grant me a willing spirit, to sustain me," we see an important distinction. What we need is a responsive and teachable spirit. This process doesn't happen in the emotional realm; it happens in the volitional realm. When you are bouncing back from blowing it big time, don't wait for your emotions to click in. Willful choices of faith keep you moving ahead in your walk with God. The pertinent question is not "How do you feel?" but "Are you willing?" God can even do a fresh work of grace in your life to grant you a willing spirit when

192

you don't feel willing. Ask him. Ask God to create anew, to renew, to restore, even to make you willing.

STEP 6: Resolve to Use Past Failure for Future Ministry

Look at David's expectations for the future. He looked forward and prayed:

> Then I will teach transgressors your ways,
> and sinners will turn back to you.
>
> verse 13

David wasn't making a deal here. He was not promising that if God would get him out of trouble, then he would teach transgressors as penance. Here we see evidence that God had already begun to answer his prayers. We see the effects of the Holy Spirit helping David face the future with hope. David was looking forward to a time in the aftermath of his transgression when he would be able to lead others on the path that he is about to tread. Do you realize that we are experiencing the answer to his prayer at this moment?

We are among the transgressors in David's prayer. We are learning about God's ways through the record of David's fall and through God's response to this prayer. What are his ways? The ways of a gracious God who is dealing with fallen people. God's ways with David are God's ways with us.

David foresaw that sinners would turn back to God because of his testimony. Something good would come out of the bad he had done. He looked forward to leading people back to God, even after he'd blown it big time. He still wanted to be used by God, and he humbly expected God to make that happen one day.

Does that give you hope? It should. Think about what God did for David. When he prayed this prayer, God responded. He fulfilled these requests in David's life, so much so that David went on being king. He went on to have the joy of his salvation restored and to teach transgressors God's ways. Yes, the consequences God decreed did come to pass, but God continued to help David bear them. David even went on to have another child with Bathsheba. That child, Solomon, became the next king. We can trust that what God did for King David reveals God's character. He will respond the same way to everyone who seeks his forgiveness with a broken, humble, and hopeful attitude. God is willing and able to do the same for us, too.

He has done it for me. He's done it for people all around you. Unfortunately, most people don't openly share how they've blown it big time and how God showed up to help them through. Their silence prevents them from seeing God using their failures to prevent others from falling. I still vividly remember the woman who volunteered to share her testimony concerning three abortions in her early years and the guilt and depression she struggled with decades later. That story ended up on tape and eventually allowed hundreds of women to come to grips with some deep pain in their pasts. Her boldness astounded me, but her response was most telling. She said, "Seeing God take the worst of my past and use it to help others was the most gracious and healing experience of my life."

I wish you knew the stories of people in our church. You would never guess by looking at them all the sinful things they have been involved in. Yet God has forgiven and loved them, restored and redeemed their messed-up lives. Their examples encourage me. Perhaps it's time to share a "window of your past" with a safe person who needs to know how God has worked in your life.

God, I Want to Get Back on the Playing Field

David wasn't through with his repentant meditation. He thought of even more possibilities for the future once God had done his part.

> Save me from bloodguilt, O God,
> the God who saves me,
> and my tongue will sing of your righteousness.

> O LORD, open my lips,
> and my mouth will declare your praise.
>
> verses 14–15

Do you hear what he was saying? "I want to get involved in ministry. I want to be used, to declare your praise." It takes a few readings for the Old Testament language to sink in. In today's expressions David might have said, "Oh, God, I am a fallen person who has blown it big time, but I want to get back out on the spiritual playing field again someday. If I get the chance, I want to tell others about you!"

Just because you have blown it doesn't mean you can never again be used by God. That is something to take up with him. Whatever your arena of ministry or areas of gifting, let God know that someday you hope to share, sing, teach, draw, or whatever again. Ask him. Take time to listen. Wait for God's response.

David continued:

> You do not delight in sacrifice, or I would bring it;
> you do not take pleasure in burnt offerings.
> The sacrifices of God are a broken spirit;
> a broken and contrite heart,
> O God, you will not despise.
>
> verses 16–17

When David said, "You do not delight in sacrifice," he meant that repentance wasn't about religious ritual. Some people try to get back on God's good side after they blow it by promising to start going to church every week or to read the Bible every day. That isn't the way. These verses show that religious activity is meaningless unless it's tied to an inward change of heart. David's words, "You do not delight in sacrifice, or I would bring it. You do not take pleasure in burnt offerings," did not mean that God didn't want sacrifices. He wasn't saying the system of offering the ram, the bull, the grain, that was in effect under the Old Testament law was now unimportant. He was getting at the fact that God doesn't want our religious ritual; he wants an unbroken, restored relationship. He wants our hearts to break when we realize the severity of our own sin, so that we will turn back to him. God always required blood to pay for sin, but a sacrifice without contrition is useless.

What awesome hope there is in this promise! "The sacrifices of God are a broken spirit; a broken and contrite heart, O God, you will not despise." I have learned this truth over and over again in my personal journey when I have sinned and failed miserably. Whenever I come with a broken spirit and a contrite heart, God meets me 100 percent of the time. At any moment, any day, any time, when you get absolutely honest and you are broken before God, he will make himself known. When you dare to look inside without deceit—that's contrition. When you dare to reflect in the light of God's holiness instead of the shade of your own rationalizations, that's contrition. When you admit that you are spiritually bankrupt, that you've blown it, and that you know you need him, you will become contrite. Don't be surprised if even a glimpse of your true condition causes you to cry out, "Oh, God, help me, it's far worse than I thought." That's when he will come. *He will come.* He won't wait for you to jump through six or seven hoops or perform a list of required religious rituals; he will simply show up because he sees a broken and contrite heart. Can you guess why that is? Contrition involves the act of drawing near to God. Spiritual magnetism takes over. James described it this way, "Come near to God and he will come near to you" (James 4:8a). God doesn't back away from those who come to him—no matter what they may have done.

STEP 7: Pray for Limited Fallout

This final step in the process is interesting. It is to pray for limited fallout from your failings. David knew that his sin didn't just impact him; sin never does. When I sin it impacts me, my wife, our kids, our church, and lots of other people. When you sin, it's like tossing a stone into the pool of your life. Everyone in the pool will be touched by the ripples. Your sin sets into motion countless effects you cannot track. No matter what the arena of your life—work, friendships, neighborhood, family—whatever position God has given you and whatever your level, your sin will eventually have an impact throughout that arena. It's a sad fact that the greater your visibility and potential impact, the greater the fallout. The higher your position, the more resounding will be your downfall. Whoever you are, when you blow it, it impacts a lot more people than you ever dreamed. I thank God that David included this. It gives us hope for that which is beyond our direct control but under our responsibility. He prayed:

> In your good pleasure make Zion prosper;
>   build up the walls of Jerusalem.
> Then there will be righteous sacrifices,
>   whole burnt offerings to delight you;
>   then bulls will be offered on your altar.
>
> verses 18–19

It's like he was admitting, "God, I know I have blown it. I've come clean. I've owned up to what I've done. I have asked you to forgive me and have accepted that you have. I hope to be used again." Then, almost like an afterthought, David may have remembered that the sword was never going to depart from his family. Perhaps he began wondering what was going to happen and how it was all going to play out. Who knows what he pictured when he thought about what Nathan had prophesied. "Hey, wait a second! In my lifetime, my wives, sleeping with someone close to me? I wonder who? This will happen in broad daylight? Wait, this shameful spectacle will be because of what I've done. I wonder how that's going to happen? Where will I be that I can't stop something like that from occurring?"

His train of thought brought to him mental pictures of the city he built to honor God. He began to think of Jerusalem. He thought about his enemies and their armies. Then it began to sink into him that private sins surely have a way of marring our public

197

image. He considered the implications, realizing that what he had assumed was a private moment of pleasure would be turned into a public humiliation. Those thoughts led to his humble prayer, "In your good pleasure, make Zion prosper." Zion is another name for Jerusalem, God's city, God's people. That's when he prayed that God would "build up the walls of Jerusalem."

What was he really saying? Something like, "Oh, dear God! Please don't let my sin ruin other people's lives." When he referred to the righteous sacrifices and so on, he was praying that even though he, as king of Jerusalem, had opened the door for the enemy, God would protect Jerusalem. He was asking God to minimize and redeem the damage he had invited into the lives of those under his rule. Basically he was saying, "God, please, don't let my blunder mess up other people's lives any more than it has to. And when it does, help them through it."

God will cause you to realize who may be negatively impacted down the line because of your sin. When he does, take time to think and care about them, not just yourself. Don't shy away from all the ugly possibilities. Consider carefully how your sin is hurting or might impact them. Then pray for God's protection over them. You may not be able to minimize the damage yourself. That may already be out of your control. Some innocent people may already be suffering because of you. Learn from David. Ask God to minimize the impact and redeem the fallout from your failings in the lives of others. God can answer that prayer in ways that continue long after the ripples have faded. Consider that in spite of David's shocking failure, God preserved David's place in the lineage of his own Son. Also consider what one New Testament writer had to say. He described David as "a man after God's own heart" (Acts 13:22). Jesus didn't reject the idea of having sinners in his family tree—people just like you and me.

Experiencing God as Your Forgiving Father

You're probably giving some thought to how this chapter applies to you. You may be remembering ways you've blown it in the past. You may also be realizing that you are standing near the top or have already started down a slippery slope. It may be that the words "singleness" and "purity" can't be used in the same sentence when speaking of your life right now. It may be something others would not consider a big deal, or something others easily excuse, but God's Spirit has spoken to you about it. But stop for a moment and be still. Be sensitive to the Holy Spirit of God. Ask him if there is any sin in your life that you need to address right now. If anything weighs on your spirit or if you see how this chapter might apply to you, choose to take the first step right now.

David relied on the "unfailing . . . covenant . . . love" of God. He was confident of God's forgiveness for a reason. He knew God redeems, restores, and renews life because of his covenant or promise. God's response is consistent with his character.

Andy's Story of Hope

As we close this chapter, I want to remind you that God's forgiveness is not simply for people long ago. God is willing and desiring to help ordinary, regular people like you and me who have failed badly.

When I've taught this truth in the life of our church, I've had the privilege of teaming up with brave men and women who were willing to tell their story of failure, forgiveness, and restoration.

Andy's story is a sad one with a happy ending. At an early age, he was exposed to soft pornography, and that began a pattern that would plague him the rest of his life. From the time he hit his mid-teens he was into hardcore pornography and was well on his way to becoming an addict. He figured getting married would solve the problem, but it didn't. Later he became a Christian and assumed that God would take away this addiction just as he had taken away all of his sins. It didn't happen. He was later asked to be a leader in his church and did so, all the while living with this secret life of a sexual addiction.

Andy begged God. Andy read books. Andy prayed and fasted but was unable to break the vicious cycle of the images that had been implanted in his mind. Finally, Andy unknowingly stumbled upon the principles that have been taught in this chapter. Confession was the key element in breaking the cycle in Andy's life. Andy found someone he could trust and got the secret out of the closet and into the light. It was a long journey and God did not take away the desire or solve all of Andy's problems overnight. In fact, it was a very painful journey in which Andy's wife was brought into the loop, and he shared his struggle, his fear, and his frustration with his addiction and his fear of losing her. Andy found a group of men who, like David, knew that the sin must come out into the light, be confessed, and dealt with completely and honestly.

Over the next few years Andy also resolved to use his past failure as a platform for future ministry. He willfully chose to risk his reputation as a leader in the church by going public with his past addiction and his victory over it.

I wish you could have sat in our church when Andy went before hundreds of people and shared his story with his wife seated in the first row. With a broken voice and tears streaming down his cheeks, he told of the pain of his past and the victory that had come through the long journey of repentance, confession, and restoration. Our church now has about four to five groups of men that meet regularly for overcoming sexual addiction because Andy came clean. In fact, he has now taken the ministry into other cities, knowing how difficult it is for men to get help with those closest to them.

I share this story because it touches on the raw nerves of what must occur in all of our hearts when we deal radically with sin. You've heard the seven steps outlined in Psalm 51. You know that David sinned and was forgiven and restored by God. But there is still the fear of what others will think and that gnawing sense that maybe God won't do for you what he's done for others. Andy's story reminds me, and I hope you, that God will not only forgive but is intent on restoring. It reminds me that when people come clean, I don't think less of them; I actually think more of them.

I sat in wonder as Andy shared his story with our entire church, but I had no sense that people thought less of Andy because he was honest and up front about where he had failed. So let me encourage you. Take the step that God is moving you to take. Walk through the following steps now as life lessons to be followed. Step by step, ask the Holy Spirit to give you the grace and the courage and the faith to do what you know is right. And know that with the help of God's Word, his Spirit, and his people, you too can be forgiven, cleansed, and restored. In all likelihood God will use the very thing that has brought so much pain in your life to serve as an instrument of grace and healing in the lives of others.

Prayer

I encourage you to use the following prayer as a place to begin in allowing God to apply the truth of Psalm 51 to your life.

Father in heaven, I ask you right now to please help my heart be tender because I know that sin makes it hard. Please let the blood of Jesus cover all my sins. Let me know if there is some area where you want me to enter into the process described in this chapter. Please give me eyes to see the truth about areas where I may need to apply these seven steps. Please make me sensitive to your Holy Spirit that I might not excuse that which is unholy.

God, I admit my human condition. I admit I often try to deny, blame, and excuse my sin away. I also realize that you want me to come clean, own my sin, and allow you to work in my spirit and my life to process it your way. Lord, if I'm tempted to minimize sinful behavior, please don't let me fall for that. I know there's no health there. Whenever I blow it, please let me come back to this place and trust you to do what I cannot. Lord, continue to do your work of cleansing and forgiveness. Please help me be honest.

God, I know I need more than seven steps. I can't do this on my own. I need to experience your presence at my point of need. Allow your Holy Spirit to have great freedom in my heart and life. Help me cooperate with his work in me. In Jesus' name I pray. Amen!

LIFE LESSONS TO APPLY

1. Come clean.

2. Ask God's forgiveness.

3. Own responsibility for your sin.

4. Accept God's forgiveness on God's terms.

5. Request a fresh work of God's grace.

6. Resolve to use past failures for future ministry.

7. Pray for limited fallout in the lives of others.

EXPERIENCING GOD WHEN YOU'VE BLOWN IT BIG TIME

Somewhere you can turn: Psalm 51

KEY VERSES

Have mercy on me, O God,
according to your unfailing love;
according to your great compassion
blot out my transgressions.
Against you, you only, have I sinned
and done what is evil in your sight,
so that you are proved right when you speak
and justified when you judge.

Psalm 51:1, 4

7

I am with you . . .

IN TIMES
OF CONFUSION

It was 5:45 A.M. My coffee was cold, but my emotions were fried. The click of the clock reminded me that I had been staring into my coffee cup for the last forty-five minutes. Lying open on my left was my Bible. In front of me waited an open journal. I had not yet read a word from Scripture nor attempted to write down any of my swirling thoughts on the blank journal pages. Just beyond the journal, my calendar was opened to today's date and a to-do list as long as my arm. I took all of this in without even moving my head. I was numb, overwhelmed, and thoroughly confused.

I don't know if you've ever felt that way, but when confusion takes over my soul, it immobilizes me. I feel the energy drain out of my body while my motivation evaporates. The long list of to-dos looks as daunting as an insurmountable mountain range. My Bible, which so often is a source of encouragement and help, appears to be nothing more than page after page of disconnected words. My journal, which God has so often used to help me process my thoughts, remains blank because I don't even know what to think.

We all face times of confusion. Sometimes it happens because we are overextended physically, and sometimes it happens because we are simply overwhelmed by the flood of facts, demands, commitments, and questions that fill our lives. Whatever the combination of these factors, I know the results: disorder, disarray, and chaos in my soul. I don't seem to be able to think clearly enough to make even the simplest decisions. It is in times like these that I desperately need God to intervene in my life to bring clarity where confusion reigns.

So, how about you? If you had to narrow it down to one area of your life where you feel the most confusion, what would it be?

207

If you had to describe in one sentence what is causing you to be filled with those confusing thoughts, what would it be? What area of your life seems to be dominated by feelings of uncertainty and hesitancy?

Perhaps you immediately thought of an area in which you are troubled by indecision. You feel you should be clear in your choices but can't make up your mind. Do you find yourself thinking, "Should I be investing more time with my kids or is our relationship healthy right now? Should they be going to a Christian school at this stage in their life or should we be making an impact in the public system?" Are you baffled by your finances? Should you be saving more? Giving more? Investing more for the future? Have you watched the stock market for the last few years and wondered, "Should I jump in or should I stay completely out?

Or, are you concerned about some deeper, lasting issues? Do you wonder about your values as you ponder where you are and where your life is headed? Do you find yourself asking questions like, "At this stage in my marriage, why do I feel so much confusion, tension, and lack of understanding? What's going to happen to us?" Perhaps you find yourself thinking in painful, private moments, "I don't feel loved. I feel like we are moving apart, but I don't know how to get us back together." These kinds of thoughts often hover just beneath the surface of our lives, but they drain us of energy and motivation, because they remind us that down deep we simply don't know what to do.

Confusion can also develop in spiritual areas. Have you had a close friend die of cancer recently and begun to question, "How could a good God let this happen?" Or have you been so busy coping with the aftershocks of the terrorist attacks of September 11 that you haven't taken time to ponder the deeper theological issues that you know are important but that you also know will leave you with more questions and concerns? It's hard not to ask, "Where is the world going? Why didn't God intervene?" Left to themselves, these subtle, chaotic thoughts will invade your mind and create a cloud of confusion that will immobilize you.

God understands that confusing times come in our lives. He is certainly not surprised when they arise. During times of confusion, God wants us to experience the leading of the Holy Spirit that will bring us to clarity. Often, times of confusion, doubt, unrest, vagueness, and disorder are actually God's signals to us that he wants to take us to a new level in our relationship with him and with others.

So, let me ask you, before we continue, in what arena of your life are you experiencing the most confusion? I ask that not simply as a rhetorical question. I long for you to identify areas of confusion as clearly as possible so that the pages that will follow can minister to you in a specific and powerful way.

Symptoms of Confusion

It's hard to get going in any direction if you're not sure where to go, isn't it? You become unmotivated, paralyzed, and neutralized. Groups don't get things done and people don't move very fast or very well unless they have clear purpose and direction. These undermining factors are like strong lines attached between a ship and the wharf. No matter how important the voyage, how strong the engines, or how willing the captain—if the vessel is still tied to the dock, the journey cannot proceed. As a pastor, I talk to people all the time who have tremendous potential and resources yet their lives are going nowhere. The reason? Complete inner turmoil and chaos. They are tied to the dock.

Two Ways to Clear Up Confusion

How do we clear up confusion, cut the lines, and set sail on a life of godly adventure? I think there are two practical ways. Teachers, coaches, and consultants all use these two approaches to clear up confusion.

1. Reduce Complexity

Those who are in the business world know the old acronym, KISS—**Keep It Simple Stupid.** Things can get so complex that no one knows what's going on. On a football team that runs a complicated offense, what's the first thing a coach does when the number one quarterback gets injured? He radically simplifies the playbook, because the key to effectiveness is to execute a few things well. Well, one way to increase effectiveness is to reduce complexity. Think again about that area of confusion in your life. On a scale of 1 to 10 (10 representing a very high level), how much complexity characterizes that area? What would happen if you simplified that part of your life?

Over the years I have observed many people (myself included) who unconsciously take on more and more projects without keeping track of the fact that we are also allowing our lives to become increasingly complex. Before long, we serve on four committees at church, chauffeur the children to three after-school practices a day, and take on that big new project at work, all while adjusting to the stress of a new baby at home! Many of us live one unexpected complication away from complete meltdown. I realize that modern life is complex, but we don't have to live that close to chaos. I can't tell you how many times in my life I've taken a look in the rearview mirror and simply decided, "I'm involved with too much, trying to do too much, with too many people!" Theresa and I then sit at the kitchen table and reprioritize our lives, our schedules, and the involvements of our children. We take out the sharp carving knife of priorities and start cutting away everything that doesn't fit what we have decided is best in our lives. The process may be painful at first, but we have found that merely tweaking our schedule will rarely produce clarity. Sometimes you simply have to accept that life has become so complex that you are not longer able to do the most important things that must be done. Significant reductions must take place. So, I ask you, where might you "keep it simple, stupid"? Identify at least one unnecessary complication and KISS it good-bye!

2. Increase Clarity

I use the acronym GBTTB to describe a second great tool coaches, counselors, and consultants use. Don't look in your business management books for that one—I made it up. GBTTB stands for: **Get Back to the Basics.** When things are confusing, we can no longer describe in simple terms what we are trying to accomplish in that area. We've forgotten the goal. That's when we have to get back to the basics, the primary principles. Vince Lombardi, the great Packer coach, was famous for his commitment to clarity. He started every football season the same way. He brought out an oblong ball and said to these professional athletes, "This, gentlemen, is a football." Talk about back to the basics! Then the team spent the first two weeks doing nothing but learning again how to block and tackle.

My college coach was a close friend of John Wooden of UCLA, whose teams won ten national basketball championships. Wooden is one of the all-time excellent teachers, coaching some of the greatest athletes in the country. During the first practice of the season, he met the team in the locker room, took off his shoes, took out a white sock and showed the players how to put the sock on properly. He did this because he knew the vital importance of starting with the basics. He told them, "If you put it on wrong and there's a fold, you may get a blister; if you get a blister, you may miss a game; if you miss a game, we might lose a game; if we lose a game, we might not win another national championship." It all goes back to the basics, in football, in business, and in life.

Basics of Life from Moses' Memoirs

When people are confused about God, about life, and about relationships, I often observe that the remedy could best be found in a personal coach, counselor, or consultant to help them get back to the basics. We all tend to drift into complexity and overextension, which produces confusion. What we all need from time to time is a wise counselor or coach to help us relocate the basics. God has used Christian counselors to do this for me in my marriage and coaches to do this for me in my athletic career. God has used consultants to do this for us as a church as we hit various growth plateaus and simply couldn't discern what our next steps should be. Let's face it, we all get confused at multiple junctures in our lives. What we need is wisdom and discernment to know where we are, where we need to go, and how to get there.

The key to getting help is choosing the right coach, counselor, or consultant. Getting back to the basics is the answer, but you have to trust the person who is going to give you direction. That's why I'm so excited about this chapter and the ways that Moses fits exactly the profile of the kind of consultant we have been discussing. Moses is a man who gives us wise counsel and serves as an excellent example of how to get back to basics. He is a man whom God called his friend (see Exod. 33:11, Num. 12:8, Deut. 34:10). This is a man the Old Testament describes as the humblest person in the world. He spent time before the very face of God and personally received the Ten Commandments.

It there's anyone who can tell us how life ought to work and show us where we are during times of confusion, it's Moses. He spent the first part of his life learning the wisdom of the greatest civilization of his day. Moses lived as a prince of Egypt. He knew what a life of luxury could provide and what it lacked. Then, for the next forty years, Moses lived in isolation and contemplation. He tended flocks in the desert and learned the Sinai wilderness like the back of his hand. He was prepared by God to be a servant. He was trained to think deeply and to know the ways of the Almighty.

Then, for the remaining forty years of his life, Moses was empowered by God for special service. He led the children of Israel and saw God work mighty miracles: part the Red Sea, provide a daily supply of manna for forty years, send showers of quail, and supply gushing water out of a rock in the wilderness.

Moses was called to lead a rebellious people. He faced times of overwhelming confusion and doubt as they resisted his leadership. He experienced times of overextension and exhaustion as the people came to him from morning to night, demanding his personal attention. Moses was a man who knew God, who saw his power, who led his people, and who, unfortunately, also had the unpleasant task of spending forty years in the desert with a people who refused to believe God's promises. During this time, Moses gained an amazing amount of wisdom. He experienced what the writer of Ecclesiastes describes by the statement, "The heart of the wise is in the house of mourning" (Eccles. 7:4). Imagine leading a group of nearly two million people as they traveled and wandered in the wilderness for forty years.

Moses led as God punished one generation and prepared the next. God promised the adult generation that they would all die before their descendants entered the Promised Land. Given these facts, I estimate that Moses probably presided over about 1.2 to 1.8 million funerals. He lived in the house of mourning for forty years. This not only made him someone who heard from God and lived in God's presence, but it also made him a realist. He knew as much about death and dying as anyone has ever learned. He became trained in every aspect of life. He developed by long experience his skills as a wise consultant. You and I could not find a more qualified counselor to help us find our way through confusing times!

God eventually had Moses pen the highlights of what he learned in this journey with God and his people in the seventeen verses that make up Psalm 90. This is the only psalm that we are aware of that Moses wrote. In it we get the *CliffsNotes* to life. In this brief psalm, Moses gathered the wisdom of God and applied it in cryptic form to allow people like you and me to get back to the basics. I know of no other psalm that has ministered more to me in my times of confusion. Whether my condition has come from emotional exhaustion, physical overextension, or complexity in relationships; it never fails to bring me back to the basics and give me clarity about where I am, what God wants me to do, and how he wants me to get there. In the pages that follow, you will see that this psalm divides into six clear basics about life. I've organized it so that I can give you the basic about life followed by a diagnostic question that will help you analyze where you are, where you need to be, and where God wants to take you. I pray that Psalm 90 will become a road map for the rest of your life, steering you from confusion, bringing clarity, and keeping you focused on the basics!

Psalm 90

Get Back to the Basics of Life

Do you want to clear away all the debris? Do you need to get clear about decisions, finances, people, eternity, marriage, parenting, and singleness—anything that's causing confusion, immobilizing your life, and paralyzing your soul? Do you want to get back to the basics, the blocking and tackling of life itself? Psalm 90 shows us how. In just seventeen verses Moses gives us six of the most basic truths of life, all directly from God.

In this section, I've identified six basic truths about life that will help bring clarity to our situations. I've turned each one of Moses' basics into a diagnostic question. Asking and answering these six diagnostic questions will help you identify the core issue behind your confusion and provide a new perspective. As you learn these six basics from Psalm 90 and apply the questions, God will help you decrease the complexity in your life and increase the clarity. You can move from being confused today to possibly seeing your life, your future, your decisions, and your relationships more clearly than you have ever seen them before. God understands how difficult and disturbing life can be when we lack clarity. So, why not take a moment right now and ask him to give you insight and wisdom into your own situation before you read this section. To follow are six basic life lessons from Moses' Memoirs.

214

BASIC 1: God Is Great!

Moses begins with the most fundamental truth of all of life. He begins with God! God is great. Moses calls us as people in the midst of a complex world to stop and remember, first and foremost, who God is. If we are foggy about God, all of life will be confusion and chaos. Moses describes God's greatness in the first two verses:

> Lord, you have been our dwelling place
> throughout all generations.
> Before the mountains were born
> or you brought forth the earth and the world,
> from everlasting to everlasting you are God.
>
> verses 1–2

The first word "Lord," as used here, is not God's covenant name, *Yahweh*. Rather, Moses uses his title *Adonai*, which means Creator, ruler, and sovereign. The phrase "dwelling place" means refuge. Moses is reminding us, "God has always been our intimate place of safety in the midst of opposition." He's telling God, "You have been the one who has cared, with fatherly, sheltering love. You have been our shield amidst all the pressure, the attacks. You have been in the cloud by day and the pillar of fire by night." His phrasing reveals in simple language some of the amazing aspects of God's nature. God is not only transcendent, but also imminent, personal, loving, and approachable. Moses looked back and saw God as great, but also as a safe refuge; not just in his own time, but through all generations. He recognized God as eternal, having no beginning and no end.

When Moses said, "You are God" he used the Hebrew word *El*. This third title or name for God is significant because of the cultural environment. The nation of Israel was on its way to take over the land of the Canaanites, who believed in many gods. One of their gods was El. According to Canaanite beliefs, El had a son named Baal. Their religion taught that Baal usurped his father.

Baal was the fertility god. The Canaanites practiced the most perverted anti-God religion, even sacrificing their children and participating in vulgar acts of worship. They honored Baal as the one who brought fertility, in reproduction and in agriculture. When Moses calls God *El*, Moses is saying God is the one superior God, and Baal is no competition.

The first basic of life is getting clear on who God is. In these two short verses, Moses has given us an accurate and biblical view of the God that we worship. Note all that Moses has captured in these brief statements:

✓ God is Creator, "he brought forth the earth and the world."
✓ God is personal, willing to be "ours" in relationship.
✓ God is eternal, "from everlasting to everlasting."
✓ God is superior to all other gods—there is no competition or rival to his power and majesty.
✓ God is loving, a protector, refuge, and lover of our souls.

Are You Rightly Related to God?

The first diagnostic question each of us needs to ask when we are confused is, *"Am I rightly related to God?"* To clarify further, "Am I rightly related, not to my idea of God, but to the God of the universe, who is holy, pure, eternal, compassionate, and king over all time and eternity? In other words, does God hold the same place in my heart that he holds in the universe? Is he my infinite reference point? Do my time, my thinking, my schedule, my priorities, and my money revolve around God and his will for my life? If the answer is "no," it may well explain why you experiencing significant confusion in your life. When we are rightly related to God, he provides perspective. But when we forget who we are worshiping and gradually cease to see him in the same role in our hearts that he carries out in the universe, we are bound to experience growing perplexity.

Not long ago I had a chance to listen to a speaker who ministers among a group of intellectuals, some of whom work at MIT and the Pentagon. He told a story about his visit with a skipper of

216

a nuclear submarine. The captain explained to him that his vessel could only stay underwater for ninety days. It wasn't because they ran out of food, water, or fuel. They had to resurface to get rightly aligned with the North Star. He said that these submarines carry missiles that could destroy the earth; therefore their calibrations have to be exact. While a submarine is underwater, the magnetic forces of the earth affect it. After ninety days have passed, those magnetic effects have the potential to alter the navigational aids considerably. Therefore, they must surface so their antenna can lock onto the North Star, to make sure they are rightly aligned with that true reference point. That's the only way to know the missiles would go exactly on target if—God forbid—they ever were ordered to fire them.

If the most sophisticated equipment on the planet has to come up to get realigned with a true reference point, doesn't it make sense that people need to find a true spiritual north and realign their lives to that? Do you have a North Star? Could the confusion in your life be a result your not being rightly related to God? Could it be that you are so busy, running after so many things, trying to get this relationship worked out and that deal sealed, that you haven't surfaced to take a reading on God and align your life with him? Are you rightly related to God? *When you are, here's what happens: you move from being perplexed to getting perspective.* When you're rightly related to God you look at life from his vantage point. That gives you perspective. You know what perspective does? It eliminates confusion.

So, how about you? Are you rightly related to God? Have you come to the point where you have received Jesus Christ as your personal savior to pay for your sins and give you eternal life? Or, as a believer already, is your relationship with God the primary focus of your life? If not, why not pause right now to ask and answer the first diagnostic question before the gentle presence of the Holy Spirit—"Am I rightly related to God?" Then respond to what he shows you, so that your life might be realigned with the personal, all-powerful, infinite reference point of the universe.

BASIC 2: Life Is Short

> You turn men back to dust,
>   saying, "Return to dust, O sons of men."
> For a thousand years in your sight
>   are like a day that has just gone by,
>   or like a watch in the night.
> You sweep men away in the sleep of death;
>   they are like the new grass of the morning—
> though in the morning it springs up new,
>   by evening it is dry and withered.
>
> verses 3–6

Second basic—life is short. Moses led probably close to two million people who wandered through the desert, waiting to die. Based on the population by my best estimate Moses probably oversaw over one hundred funerals every day for forty years. Every time the nation moved camp, they left behind a large cemetery. One by one, an entire generation died off. No wonder Moses wrote, "You turn men back to dust saying return to dust, sons of men" (literally, sons of Adam). He gave us three quick word-pictures to show us how short life is:

1. "For a thousand years in your sight are like a day that's just gone by, or like a watch in the night." Military watches traditionally ran four hours.
2. "You sweep men away in the sleep of death." The word means a torrential rain; death resembles a flash flood that wipes out everything in its path.
3. People's lives are "like the new grass of the morning—though in the morning it springs up new, by evening it is dry and withered."

I went to Israel a few years ago. There we saw plains where the grass comes up green in the morning, but certain times of the year, hot, dry winds come up and kill off the new grass within hours.

You can look at those fields in the morning, and they're green; that evening they're brown. That's a picture of how short life is.

Recently, several people I've been close to and loved have died. One of them was a middle-aged man named Bruce Barnett, who died of cancer. I'll never forget what he told the people of our church when he spoke about his experience. He said, "We are all terminal. I am obviously terminal—but so are you. The only question is, 'When?'" There was a sober silence in the room. We all know this intellectually, but when someone close to you says it in front of a large group of people, including his wife and two children sitting in the third row, it really hits home. But we don't like to hear it. Down deep in our hearts we say, "I've got time." We make all kinds of mental excuses that we will deal with these major spiritual issues when things calm down. Procrastination is the word of the day, and as we all know, things never calm down.

Moses buried well over a million people. He understood life is short. He faced daily what we try to avoid. I don't know what you procrastinate about, but I do know one thing I procrastinate about—thinking seriously about dying. We live like we are going to live forever, don't we? But the only certain day human beings can count on is the day they cross the line from time into eternity. That is something most people don't plan for; most don't even want to think about it. But Moses puts it right in our faces.

We were made for both time and eternity, but life is short. The most important question you can ever ask yourself is, *Are you ready to die?* Are you? If you knew with absolute certainty that in exactly thirty days, at precisely 11:00 A.M., your heart would stop, would you live any differently between now and that date? Is there anybody you'd call to apologize to? Is there anything that needs to get done? Are there any areas in your life that need to be shored up or refocused? Would you watch as much TV? Would you spend as much time amusing yourself, killing time? Or would you live with a purpose and a plan? I would like to be so generous as to guarantee you thirty more days to live, but I can't. I can't guarantee it for me and I can't guarantee it for you. I don't know if you will live that long. Life is short and you don't know when it's going to be over in the here and now. That's why we dare not dodge the implications of this basic understanding of life. *Remem-*

bering that our time is short moves us from a life characterized by pro-crastination to a life characterized by priorities. Much of our confusion flows from that nagging sense of guilt that accompanies a sched-ule filled with the urgent rather than the truly important. I chal-lenge you to stop right now and ponder what you are doing with your life. If you would honestly live a lot differently in the next thirty days if you knew they were your last, why not start living that way right now?

BASIC 3: Sin Is Serious

After graphically reminding us of our mortality, Moses now explains why life is short—why death is part of our future. In verses 7 through 10 he states emphatically that *sin is serious.* You see, death was not in the original plan. God designed human beings in his image to enjoy fellowship with him forever. God's best was not for life to be snuffed out and cut off, but a problem arose. There was a coup on the planet; a rebellion within God's creation. Adam and Eve willfully chose to disobey God. They chose not to listen to his word or enjoy the perfect environment that he had created for them. Instead, they reasoned that they knew bet-ter. They were deceived and then chose to rebel against their good and holy creator.

God loved the people he created far more than we love our own children. But disobedience created a chasm between a holy God and his sinful creatures. Their choice to rebel produced in God an emotion with which we can readily identify—anger. That's right, sin made God very, very angry. Not bad anger, but a just and righteous wrath. If these words sound strange, let me give you a quick picture that will provide a sense of what sin did to our relationship with God and why it produces these deep emo-tions of righteous anger in his heart.

Imagine if you will, holding a newborn baby in your arms. It's your baby, a child you deeply love. You have anticipated this baby, prepared for it, and loved it long before it arrived. You know that your home and your life will be completely different with the addition of this new life. As you are walking out of the hospital, a stranger runs by and snatches the baby out of your arms. Then, before you can shout or respond, that stranger stops a few feet away and violently throws the child down onto the sidewalk. As you watch that precious life snuffed out, your own dreams and part of your own life also die. Please forgive the graphic nature of this illustration, but the sense of horror, rage, and loss that you would immediately feel is only a small glimmer of the anger and wrath that God felt when sin invaded his perfect creation and destroyed his relationship with Adam and Eve. You see, God is our Father, and sin brought death into the world.

God reacts with justified anger and wrath. Why? Why would that mom and dad be angry if someone threw their baby down to its death? Why do we get angry when one of our kids endangers his or her life by running out into traffic? Because when we love someone, we get angry over anything that threatens his or her well-being. We get angry because we love the one who is endangered by the wrongdoing.

Read slowly and thoughtfully what Moses wrote,

> We are consumed by your anger
>   and terrified by your indignation.
> You have set our iniquities before you,
>   our secret sins in the light of your presence.
> All our days pass away under your wrath;
>   we finish our years with a moan.
> The length of our days is seventy years—
>   or eighty, if we have the strength;
> yet their span is but trouble and sorrow,
>   for they quickly pass, and we fly away.
>
> Who knows the power of your anger?
>   For your wrath is as great as the fear that is due you.
>
> Psalm 90:7–11

221

When we are called before a holy God, there is no place to run or hide. All our days pass away under his just wrath and anger. We come to the end groaning . . . Life is short: We measure the length of our days by seventy or eighty years, but longevity is largely out of our control. Yet what is the day-to-day content of life? Trouble and sorrow haunt us. Our years quickly pass, then afterward, what? We fly away. Fly away to what? To judgment.

When I read this passage, I circled these words in the text: consumed, terrified, moan, trouble, sorrow, and quickly pass. Those are not happy headlines. Then, I put boxes around these words: anger, indignation, wrath. Since sin entered the world, relationships have not been right, the planet has not been right, people don't treat one another rightly. Our sin has separated us from a holy God who has just wrath and anger toward our sin. He is holy; therefore his indignation must be appeased.

Let me ask you, do you take sin seriously? I mean, do you tend to think about and describe sin with terms like mistake, slipup, and little error? Have you gotten the foggy notion that God is a lot like Santa Claus? He will understand. I mean, nobody is perfect. What's a little white lie, what's the big deal about a little stealing, a little cheating? Hey, what's the problem with sleeping around? After all, we love each other. No! That is not God's take on sin. The Bible says sin is so serious and God's character so holy, that he demands that the sins we commit in this life be judged. They have already been judged. The verdict for each one of us is: guilty. The punishment is death.

Galatians 6:7–8 says, "Do not be deceived: God cannot be mocked. A man reaps what he sows. The one who sows to please his sinful nature, from that nature will reap destruction; the one who sows to please the Spirit, from the Spirit will reap eternal life." These words are sobering. They are also unpopular and hard to hear. But each one of us knows the pain and suffering that sin has brought into our lives. Who reading this page right now hasn't been hurt, rejected, afflicted, or even abused by someone else's selfishness and sin. And in our most honest moments, we also know that our lies, greed, and lusts have done untold damage to others.

222

When sin prevails, people get hurt. You know what all this damage to people and relationships represents? It's the fruit of sin. When people sow distrust, dishonesty, and disrespect, they reap multiplied bitterness, anger, and resentment. You know what that does? It shatters relationships, it makes businesses go downhill, and it causes people to run and hide, getting lost in a world of videos and virtual reality—anything but dealing with the real stuff.

Sin is serious business, yet we live in a world of pervasive denial. That's why some people can't get in their car without turning on the tape player, CD player, or the radio for music and sports talk. That's why some people click on the stereo or the TV the moment they get in the house. They've got to have noise, food, or amusement to drown out the cries of a guilty conscience. I do it; you do it; we all do it to some degree. We turn to almost anything to sedate the unrest in our souls.

When was the last time you got quiet and said, "God, search me, and know my heart. Try me and know my thoughts. See if there be any sinful way in me. Show me bitterness, show me resentment, and show me where my thoughts are less pure than you want them to be. Point out to me where there could be any block between me and you, or me and another person." You know why we don't do that very often? Because we inherently know how quickly God's Spirit can locate those sins we have been denying or covering up. We mistakenly choose to tolerate sin rather than invite God's continual examination and cleansing.

When you take sin seriously, you will find yourself tending to avoid every manner of pollution, spiritually, mentally, and emotionally. You'll be careful of what comes out of your mouth, what goes into your mind, where your hands go, and where your affections lie. If you truly take sin seriously, you will run from sin and pursue purity. And as you do that, an amazing thing will start to happen—life will get clearer and less chaotic.

In fact, one major cause of confusion in decision making and relationships is the presence of unresolved sin in our lives. When we are in situations and relationships that are not pure, we will not be able to see clearly to make decisions. It's like trying to see out of a fogged-up car window. That's a picture of how a lot of people are living their lives. They are peering ahead as they move

223

along, but it is real foggy. They see some light coming through, but they don't really know what's out there, they don't know what perils are before them, they are confused. Sin fogs up our ability to see clearly and proceed rightly in life. Sin needs to be cleaned away.

I can't tell you the number of people who have approached me after a sermon to express confusion about God's direction in their lives. They describe their inability to hear God's voice in order to know what to do in a specific relationship, job opportunity, or some other personal area of their lives. So often, as I've asked some questions about their time in God's Word, their lifestyle, and their attitudes, they eventually reveal they are actually involved in blatant sin. Usually I will find that their hearts are filled with bitterness and resentment, or they are feeding their minds on things that are egregious to God. So as you seek to get clarity and direction in your life, Moses would have you ask yourself, "Am I taking sin seriously?"

BASIC 4: Wisdom Is Essential

> Teach us to number our days aright,
> that we may gain a heart of wisdom.
>
> verse 12

Note the progression in the first eleven verses: God is great, life is short, and sin is serious. Then Moses provided the next logical life lesson: wisdom is essential. He cried out for help. In verse 11, he asked a searching rhetorical question, "Who knows the power of your anger? For your wrath is as great as the fear that is due you." I imagine he was thinking back over all the funerals he had conducted. Maybe he replayed the scene of when Korah rebelled and the ground opened up to swallow him, his followers, their wives, and children (Num. 16). Moses had seen what happened when people were belligerent and unforgiving, when they began

224

to worship idols. He saw how God responded with powerful judgment. Moses was deeply conscious of what we pass over lightly: that God is holy. He doesn't mess around with sin. When Moses reflected on the holiness of God, the power of his wrath against sin, and the people he had to deal with, he realized they were in a jam. Like us, Moses was acutely aware of how difficult it is to live a righteous life in a fallen and sinful world. He realized he needed help, and he models for us exactly how to get it. He prayed.

Listen to his prayer in verse twelve, "Teach us to number our days" (v. 12). Because life is short, sin is serious, and God is holy, Moses realized we need God to teach us to know how to live and use our time wisely. We need a heart of wisdom, so we can live life God's way. Wisdom is not just intellectual ability. In the Hebrew language, the word translated as "wisdom" involves the idea of skill. The Old Testament describes the wise as those who know how God wants us to live and who exercise skill in living that way.

Wisdom is the supernatural ability to understand how to live your life according to God's design. God has our highest and best in mind; but how do we experience that in life, day by day? That is exactly what Moses is asking God to show him. Godly wisdom hears the revelation from God's Word and then seeks moment by moment and day by day to make it work in real life, in relationships, and within the community of God's people. This kind of wisdom involves thought, planning, scheduling, and priority choices so our actions, our speech, our financial dealing, our use of time, and our family relationships reflect God's design as revealed in the Word.

Numbering Our Days

What does it mean to "number our days"? In modern terms, Moses was praying, "Lord, teach us to count down our days. Teach us to make the best use of our time, talents, and treasure in the light of eternity." To bring the power of this request home, I've done a little math that's helped me get my arms around the concept of numbering my days. For example, if you are twenty-five years old today, you would have 16,275 days left to live in order to reach Moses' idea of typical lifespan—seventy years. If

225

you are thirty-five years old today, you would have 12,775 days left to live if you live to seventy. If you are forty-five—which hits close to home for me—you'd have 9,175 days. That's less than ten thousand days. If you're fifty-five, you'd be down to 5,575 days. And if you're sixty-five years old, you'd have less than 2,000 days of time on the planet before turning seventy. It's not all that long, is it?

When you learn to number your days, you'll find priorities grow in importance. Ask yourself this fundamental question: *"Am I spending my life or investing it?"* Let me ask you: Have you bought into spending your time just amusing yourself or are you investing your life into something worthwhile? Is there a sense that since life is brief, you want it to count? Are you fully engaged in your life, recognizing that you are living before the watchful gaze of God, who is holy? Do you regularly think about giving a detailed personal account for your life to the one who entrusted you with it? Does the real possibility of judgment cross your mind? These questions may make us feel squeamish. They ought to. You may feel like this is bad news. Actually, it is bad news, but people tend not to appreciate good news until we get the bad news straight.

We live in a time when some people think that technology is going to solve all our problems and cure all diseases. We may applaud scientific advances, but technology in the hands of immoral, unwise people can be used more for evil than for good. Developments in the use of nuclear power have created the potential for almost unlimited energy, yet those same technologies create bombs that threaten the lives of millions. We need to wake up and realize that in spite of our supposed enlightened civilization, more people have been slaughtered this century alone than in all the history of mankind. We are so technically proficient, so advanced, so sophisticated that Stalin was able to kill as many as fifty million people, Hitler slaughtered six million Jews, and on it goes. There are places all over the world where human beings are annihilating other human beings with the help of advanced technology. Sure, we can get on the Internet; we have penicillin and MRIs—all tools for good or weapons for evil. Does our technology really count for much if we are not using it wisely?

226

My point? We need to make it a priority to develop wisdom. I will never forget a lesson from one of my mentors, Professor Howard Hendricks. Some of the students who wanted to learn from this godly man pushed to get some time with him. We ended up meeting every Wednesday for lunch.

He asked, "What's the biggest issue in your life?"

We responded, "School—the pressure, the confusion of trying to earn a living, be good fathers, good husbands, and somehow maintain our walk with God." Then we asked a series of questions that we hoped he would answer.

"You seem real disciplined," someone observed. "How do you set priorities and schedules?"

Someone else added, "How do you decide what to do, what not to do?"

I asked, "How do you make time to spend an hour with the Lord every morning?"

We seemed to be saying together, "Dr. Hendricks, you have lot of wisdom. We want to get it." So he took us through a twelve- or thirteen-week series of lunches where we just opened the Bible as we ate our brown-bag lunches. I can still hear him crunching on an apple as he shared with us a lifetime worth of godly insight.

Much of our time during those weeks was taken up by Dr. Hendricks's responses and observations about personal problems we posed to him. During one of those lunches, I decided to share an issue that had created continual confusion in my life. I said something like, "Dr. Hendricks, I have an ongoing struggle in my life. Whenever I make progress in self-discipline, I almost immediately find myself getting self-righteous. I quickly get to be a jerk and can't even stand myself. I spend time in the morning praying and memorizing verses, but I find myself thinking I'm better than everybody else. I know that isn't right. But when I was undisciplined, I felt guilty, confused, and I didn't know where I was going. I'm wondering if you can help me with this vicious circle."

I will never forget his answer. He said, "Gentlemen, you need to understand two things if you are going to go anywhere in life. Few people understand these, but you'd better get it." I got my pen out and took down these words:

227

1. There is nothing you can ever do to get God to love you any more than he does right now.
2. There is nothing you can ever do to get God to love you less.

In Light of Grace, What Kind of Person Does God Want Us to Be?

Your performance is irrelevant when it comes to God loving and accepting you. God's reasons are called grace. Now, in light of that grace you better sit down some day and decide: Who do you want to be? What kind of man, what kind of woman do you want to be by the time you hit seventy, seventy-five, eighty, or whenever you cross the gate and stand before God? Do you want to be a godly person? Do you want to be a parent that raises good kids as best you know how? Do you want to be a person whose life has significance? Do you want to leave behind people who talk authentically about the positive impact of your life?

Whatever you aspire to be, you must make that a priority in your life. Then organize your time and activities to work toward those priorities. Put those in your schedule. Discipline yourself, day by day, to pursue those things. But don't pursue your priorities because you think you'll earn any brownie points with God but because that's who you want to be. That is the way biblical wisdom looks at life. That day, listening to Dr. Hendricks, I decided that was what I wanted to do. Those words of wisdom applied to my life brought clarity out of confusion.

You know what it means? It means you live a life of intentionality; a life that is governed by purpose and passion rather than passivity. It means you watch a lot less TV. You eat a lot less food. Appetites lose their position of control and come under the discipline of godly priorities. It means when all the rest of the world is floating downstream, you are swimming against the current.

If you live by godly priorities, you will not have a lot of company. There are not many believers who really live for God, who exercise that kind of wisdom. That's why George Barna's surveys and the Gallup Polls don't show a big difference between the divorce rate among believers and unbelievers, little difference in practicing dishonesty on the job between believers and unbe-lievers. I believe that "sameness with the world" grieves the heart of God. But our culture is powerful. We get sucked in, don't we? I do.

When you live your life wisely, you live life God's way. You start to invest your life instead of living according to the dictates of daily pressures. If you live wisely, with clearly defined priorities in keep-ing with God's Word, you will see fruitfulness. Be prepared to pay the price. Unfortunately, you may seem like an "oddball" early on, but the rewards of doing life God's way are incalculable.

BASIC 5: Mercy Is Available

> Relent, O Lord! How long will it be?
>   Have compassion on your servants.
> Satisfy us in the morning with your unfailing love,
>   that we may sing for joy and be glad all our days.
> Make us glad for as many days as you have afflicted us,
>   for as many years as we have seen trouble.
>
> verses 13–15

In the fifth basic, Moses finally got around to the good news. Up to this point, the psalm has been pretty heavy. I suppose any-one who had done so many funerals would be a realist. Moses didn't expect someone to invent a magic pill to solve life's prob-lems. He'd been around a hundred and twenty years. He knew God. He didn't just understand his holiness, he also understood the depth of his love, mercy, and compassion. Therefore, Moses said that no matter how badly you fall, or what you have done wrong, or what terrible things you've plotted in your heart, you are never outside the reach of God's mercy.

God's mercy means that you do not get what you deserve. In comparison, grace means that we get the good we do not deserve. Read the last two sentences again. They will help you understand why we need both God's mercy and God's grace. Mercy withholds the punishment we deserve while grace offers us forgiveness we don't deserve. According to God's law all sin deserves to be punished by death. However, God's nature is such that he always provides a way for human beings to avoid getting the judgment we truly deserve. In the Old Testament this provision was mediated through the blood of animals; in the New Testament God's mercy comes through the blood of Jesus Christ shed on the cross. Whenever God says, "I will forgive, I will restore, I will pick you up, I will set you free, I will wrap my arms around you, I will redeem the past . . ." these are not rewards we *deserve;* these are demonstrations of God's mercy and grace.

Listen to what Moses prayed: "Relent, O LORD! How long will it be? Have compassion on your servants. Satisfy us in the morning with your unfailing love, that we may sing for joy and be glad all our days" (Psalm 90:13–14). Why ask God for compassion and love? "So that we may sing for joy and be glad." How long? "All of our days." Then he switched to an imperative, "Make us glad for as many days as you have afflicted us, for as many years as we have seen trouble." (v. 15). Once Moses began to think about what God might do, he couldn't help but think of the nation's experiences. They had suffered in Egypt for 400 years. Why not ask for an equal time period of blessing? He was thinking in larger than human terms. His request represented his understanding of God's unlimited resources. His boldness flowed from his confidence in God's abundant generosity.

In the midst of a confusing and uncertain world, God wants you to have joy in your heart. In times of uncertainty—when relationships are going south, when finances are tight, when you don't know what the future holds or where your kid ought to go to school, or whether you even ought to have kids—he wants to give you joy. Listen carefully: *what the holiness of God demanded, the love of God provided.* What the holiness of God demanded (judgment of sin), the love of God provided (Christ). The love of God was in his Son, the second person of the Trinity who hung upon a cross for your sin and my sin. When Jesus went to the cross, all your sin, all my sin, and all the world's sin was placed on Jesus. The just wrath of God came upon him. That's why he cried out,

"My God, my God, why have you forsaken me?" There was willing division in the tri-unity of the Godhead for the first time in all eternity. You can receive pardon for your sin the moment you believe and accept the free gift of mercy that God is offering in Christ Jesus, his righteousness is transferred on to you, no matter what you have done, or how awful your past, God wants to forgive your sin today, once for all.

You are just a prayer away. That was part of Moses' attitude behind his words, "relent," "have compassion," and "satisfy us." Begin with an honest prayer for forgiveness right now. Those words Moses used express surrender, understanding, and acceptance. They are the prayer of someone ready to cooperate with God's plan, someone ready to turn away from the confusion of self-rule to the clarity of life under God's guidance.

Perhaps when I touched on the seriousness of sin, the Holy Spirit brought to mind sins in your life: resentment, unresolved issues with your ex, in-law trouble, stealing, or sexual immorality. Maybe you are hooked on internet porn or some other "secret" sin. Maybe you are planning how to leave your husband or wife. Maybe you're a young person in rebellion against your parents. Maybe you're just sick and tired of your own kids or actually find yourself treating them in ways that make you feel guilty and full of shame. Maybe your issues aren't about overt, sexual behaviors, but ones that no one else knows about. Maybe you have a reputation as a devout Christian, but you haven't cracked open the Bible in ages. You can't remember the last time you had a prolonged significant time when you sensed the Spirit of God wash you, cleanse you, and give you real intimacy with God. Maybe you're living a life of pretend.

Here's what God wants you to know. You don't have to get your act together, try harder, get disciplined, or do something good in order to encounter him right now, right where you are, today. He just wants to say, "Can I love you? Would you let me forgive you? Would you let me apply what Jesus did on the cross for you right now?"

If you are a believer, you know how it works and what to do. Why not stop right now and have an honest season of confession and let God forgive and restore you. If you are not a believer, if you are not a follower of Christ, God wants to do a miracle in your life right now. He wants to give you the gift of eternal life and put your past behind you.

It's very simple. You say, "Lord Jesus, please forgive me, save me (relent your righteous judgment of me). I want to have a right relationship with you (have compassion on me). I believe when you died on the cross you paid for my sin. Will you come into my life right now and make me a part of your eternal family?"

By doing so, you are turning from your old life and receiving a gift of forgiveness by faith. If you have never done that, I urge you to do it. It's not hard. It is not difficult; but it is significant. If you need more information or help, you should certainly find a committed Christian whose life mirrors the priorities we have been talking about. They can help you. If you can't think of how to talk to them, ask them to read this chapter and then tell them you want their counsel in putting these principles into action. If you are a believer and have prayed a prayer of repentance, I encourage you to seek out your pastor or a wise leader in your church and get the help you will need in order to continue to grow spiritually.

Although our emotional responses will vary when we experience God's forgiveness, there is a time-tested evidence of his working in our lives. That evidence is joy! Psalm 16:11 says, "In thy presence is fullness of joy. At thy right hand are pleasures forever" (KJV). It's true. The final outcome and evidence of God's work in your life is joy, even bubbling up in the midst of adverse circumstances. God's presence and power in your life always seek to produce joy. When you're experiencing the joy of the Lord, your circumstances may not change, but your perspective on them will be radically altered. Instead of being inundated with your problems, you will begin to view your problems through the grace and power of God.

One of the questions I've learned to ask myself over the years is, *Am I experiencing the joy of the Lord in my life?* It's not a "foolproof" method, but this diagnostic question helps me discern the degree to which I am allowing the Holy Spirit to lead and direct my life. When the Christian life feels like a series of "ought's," "should's," and duties to be done, I know something has happened in my heart that needs attention.

232

Though I don't want to overstate the case, I believe deep, honest, intimate, and regular seasons of prayer are the key to maintaining our experience of God's joy. I believe prayer is the most difficult, rigorous discipline—at least for me—in the Christian life. By this I mean honest prayer, not prayer on the run, not just the prayers prayed while driving in the car, or while drinking a cup of coffee, or around the dining table, not prayer that is hit or miss. I mean, prayer where you get real, you get open, and you talk to God. You pour out your heart until it is empty.

Then you stop talking and you listen for him to talk to you, and you let him love you. When he convicts you of sin, you realize that it's not because he is down on you. He does it because he wants to restore you. Remember what Moses said at the beginning about God, "You have been our shelter, our dwelling place." These words convey the meaning, "You have been the one who has held us with your arms. You have been our shield." That's what God wants to be for you. He is not down on you; he wants to give you mercy and joy.

BASIC 6: Success Is Possible

> May your deeds be shown to your servants,
>   your splendor to their children.
>
> May the favor of the Lord our God rest upon us;
>   establish the work of our hands for us—
>   yes, establish the work of our hands.
>
> verses 16–17

This final basic is very good news! Following are Moses' declarations that

✓ God is great
✓ life is short
✓ sin is serious

✓ wisdom is essential
✓ mercy is available

He closed with the assurance that success is possible. He said, "May your deeds be shown to your servants, your splendor to their children" (v. 16). The phrase literally means, "Reveal your works." He was saying, "God, let us see your work in our time. But, not just for us, reveal your splendor to our children. We all want to leave a legacy. We want to see the working of the Spirit of God in authentic power, not just in our experience but also in our kids' experience." As verse 17 goes on to emphasize, "May the favor of the LORD our God rest upon us and," get this last request, "establish the work of our hands, yes, establish the work of our hands."

This is a way of saying, "We want to know your work, your power. We want to see you. We want to encounter you in our lives and our future posterity. We don't want to live off other people's stories of what God has done for them. We don't just want to hear how God is working in other families, other places. We want it in our experience and we want to pass it on to the next generation." Even though we may not be missionaries or pastors, we can all cry out for God to establish the work of our hands. Moses' final words are amazing! He is asking God to take even the mundane and the "regular grind of life" and allow it to be used for eternal purposes. When done to honor God and with a spirit of dependency, all of the following can literally become acts of worship:

✓ the work of a mom with a baby at home
✓ the work of someone who types all day
✓ the work of someone pounding nails
✓ the work of someone trying a case or performing surgery
✓ your work, in your life, done this day for God

That's right, Moses is praying, "God, establish the work of regular everyday people, so that the glory and splendor of Yahweh might be manifest through regular people like you and me." Life doesn't have to be meaningless drudgery. Success is possible. And God will give you the grace to do it.

Moses' prayer can actually be reduced to this simple statement: "I want to know God and I want to make him known. I want to make him known not just by my lips and my words, but by my works, by how I live, how I talk, what happens at the office or on the construction site."

So how's your life going? Are you in that vicious cycle of rise, eat, work, sleep, then get up and do it again? *Or are you impacting your world for good?*

The key word here at the end of Psalm 90 is productivity. When you're really impacting your world for good, you experience the satisfaction of productivity instead of boredom and futility. TGIF (Thank God It's Friday) is a good name for a restaurant but a very poor catchphrase for a worldview. When you are living in light of Psalm 90, you will really live every day of every week productively, not just looking for the week to be over. God doesn't want you to live with a TGIF mentality. So, how do we move beyond it? We get up every day and pray what Moses prayed: "God Almighty, use me! Let me see your power today! Establish the work of my hands!" As you take on this attitude, watch out! Some interesting things just might start to happen.

Experiencing God as Your Wise Counselor

I would like you to go back to that big question I asked you at the beginning of this chapter. Where do you feel confused? Where do you need clarity in your life—vocationally, spiritually, with regard to your future or a decision? Now, ask these diagnostic questions very honestly before God.

1. Am I rightly related to God?
2. Am I prepared to die?
3. Am I taking sin seriously?
4. Am I spending or investing my life?
5. Am I experiencing the joy of the Lord?
6. Am I impacting my world for good?

As you answer these under the guidance of God's Spirit, he will create a dynamic within you that will help you think clearly. If you will then seek God's way earnestly, you will be prepared to act clearly and consistently. Little by little he will move you from confusion to clarity.

Before we end this chapter, I invite you to take some time right now to do business with God. Choose to be someone who has received mercy; one who will seek wisdom; one whose life is charting a course of success by God's standards. Please read over and then pray this prayer with me:

> *Father, we thank you that mercy is available. We don't have anything that will sustain us except you.*
>
> *Lord Jesus, I want you in my life, forgive me for my sin, come into my life. I believe you died for me in my place for my sin. Please make me the kind of man or woman you want me to be. Give me clarity to replace my confusion. May I encounter you as a gracious, loving, merciful God who has been looking for me all my life. In your name, Jesus, I pray. Amen.*

LIFE LESSONS TO APPLY

1. God is great.
2. Life is short.
3. Sin is serious.
4. Wisdom is essential.
5. Mercy is always available.
6. Success is possible.

EXPERIENCING GOD IN TIMES OF CONFUSION

Somewhere you can turn: Psalm 90

KEY VERSES

Lord, you have been our dwelling place
throughout all generations.
Before the mountains were born
or you brought forth the earth and the world,
from everlasting to everlasting you are God.
Teach us to number our days aright,
that we may gain a heart of wisdom.

Psalm 90:1–2, 12

8

GOD IS
WITH YOU
ALWAYS

I don't know about you, but I can still remember my first real, honest prayer to God. Sure, I recited "Now I lay me down to sleep" and "Thank you for this food we eat" as a little boy, but those were someone else's prayers. I'm thinking of the first time I cried out to God for myself.

My prayer came out of a time of specific, desperate, and painful need. In fact, I was in a situation that included many of the experiences we've looked at in these chapters—crisis, fear, doubt, and confusion. You see, I badly damaged my knee early in my teenage years. Except for my family, basketball and baseball meant more to me than anything in the world. The injury to my knee led to an almost complete loss of strength in my left quadriceps. I wondered if I would ever participate successfully in sports again. Over a period of two years, I visited the doctor's office every four to six weeks for shots that were supposed to dissolve the calcium deposits below my left knee. It would work for a few days, but then the lump and the pain returned.

One night, feeling completely trapped in this vicious cycle of pain and frustration, I cried out to God. I told him that if he would heal my knee, I would be willing to do anything he asked me to do. I realize that this prayer fits neatly in the foxhole prayer category, but I also think those kind of prayers are part of human nature. Because there's nothing immediate we can offer God in exchange for his help, we try to offer our future. Sometimes we mean it; often we don't.

My recollection of the event is vivid and indelible. I was sitting in a hot bath, examining my legs, when I began to remem-

241

ber the stories about Jesus I had heard as a child. Though we were not a Bible-reading family, nor even Christians by the biblical definition, we did go to church, where I had learned the basic Bible stories. As I compared my legs, there was no doubt which one had a problem. My left one had no muscle tone; it was shrunken and painful. I thought of Jesus traveling from town to town, healing people. I closed my eyes, and with all my might, I asked God to heal my leg. I reasoned that if Jesus did it back then, why couldn't he do it now? The truth is, I didn't really know who Jesus was, and I didn't really know if God cared. But I was desperate.

I'm sure you have had at least one moment in your life when out of a critical, immediate need, you cried out to God. You wondered if he really existed; and if he did, would he help you? For some of you, the answer came in a miraculous manifestation that began your journey with the living God. For others, the cry for help seemed to go unheeded, and you wondered if all those stories about Jesus were really true.

The Psalms were written by and for people just like us who desperately needed God's help at some point in their lives and even more desperately needed to encounter God.

We've walked together through some of life's most universal needs. Who doesn't suffer injustice at some time or another? Who hasn't gone through a major crisis or felt insignificant? I don't know anyone who doesn't get a little depressed now and then. All of us know something about fear. Guilt and shame are such a real part of the human experience; we've all blown it, and we all know it. Confusion seems to drift in and out of our lives like the fog along the California coast. These universal needs are what drive us to God. I wish it weren't so. I wish that on my own, when things were great, I would run to him and long to serve and please him with all my heart. But the sad fact for me, and likely for many reading these words, is that we turn to God the most when the demands, or pains, or uncertainties of life close in upon us.

As we wrap up our time together, I want you to know that God wants to meet you on a far more regular basis than when you are in need. In fact, to turn to God only when we're hurting, struggling, or confused greatly limits the quality of our relationship with God. The truth is God wants to meet us in good times and in bad. He wants to be your best friend and faithful companion. He wants to guide you, lead you, direct you, empower you, and fill you with joy beyond your wildest dreams. He's a personal God and he knows all about you. You may be attracted to him and meet him in a time of need, but his plans and desires for you go well beyond any momentary crisis.

So that raises the question, what exactly is God like? Throughout the Psalms, we received various glimpses of God that provided pieces of the puzzle but simply didn't give us the whole picture. In fact, the writer of Hebrews put it this way, "In the past God spoke to our forefathers through the prophets at many times and in various ways, but in these last days he has spoken to us by his Son, whom he appointed heir of all things, and through whom he made the universe. The Son is the radiance of God's glory and the exact representation of his being, sustaining all things by his powerful word" (Heb. 1:1–3a).

More than anything in the entire world, God wants a relationship with you. He wants so much to establish that intimate bond with you that he sent Jesus, the second person of the Trinity, to reveal to you and me what he's really like. The apostle John tells us that Jesus came to reveal the Father, full of truth and grace (see John 1:14). On the night before Jesus' death, one of his disciples asked him, "Show us the Father." Jesus replied simply and directly, "Anyone who has seen me has seen the Father" (see John 14:8–14). Jesus is God's clearest and most complete communication of himself to us. We will never know God better than we can know him in Jesus Christ. Everything we have learned about God through the Psalms, we can also see illustrated and incarnated in Jesus. That's because, as Hebrews puts it, God spoke "*through* the prophets at many times and in various ways," but he eventually and completely communicated himself "*by* his Son."

So if we want to experience God today, we must get to know Jesus Christ! Notice how Jesus fits the character of God as illustrated in each of the Psalms we've studied.

Psalm 73—Jesus Is the Sovereign Lord

In Psalm 73 we learned that God is the sovereign king of the universe and is in control of all of life—even when we encounter injustice. The Bible also makes it clear that the character of Jesus, the Messiah, will be marked by a passion for justice and divine authority over creation (see Isa. 9:6–7; Luke 4:16–21). The New Testament describes Jesus as one who will be exalted as King of Kings and Lord of Lords, before whom every knee will eventually bow in recognition of his supreme identity (see Phil. 2:2–5). Jesus wants you to know that when you encounter injustice and get a raw deal, he will be with you always. He will never leave you or forsake you. He understands what it's like to be unjustly treated. He who knew no sin bore our sins and understood the humiliation of getting a raw deal at the hands of evil men. He understands what you are going through and has promised that he will be there with you if you let him. When the King of the universe says to you, "I am with you always," that means you're in the best company.

Psalm 23—Jesus Is the Good Shepherd

In Psalm 23 we learned that God would be our shepherd in the midst of crises. That he would accompany us through the valley of the shadow of death. God will protect us when life's uncertainties and difficulties surround us. If there was any doubt about the identity of the shepherd, Jesus ended that when he claimed the title of Good Shepherd (John 10). Jesus desires that you experience what he can do as your good shepherd. He wants to lead you, guide you, and protect you. He will give you direction, accompany you through life's transitions, and comfort you during life's hard knocks. As sheep know their shepherd's voice and he knows their every need, so Jesus wants to be recognized by us as the one who knows us better than we know ourselves. He knows how we feel and what we're going through. He is instantly available to lift us if we've fallen. He remains close, even during those times when the darkness consumes our soul. He is a faithful provider who promises to meet our needs and even commands us to trust him for our daily bread. For a sheep, nothing conveys greater comfort than to hear the Good Shepherd say, "I am with you always."

Psalm 139—Jesus Is Your Creator

In Psalm 139 we learned that God understands our feelings of insignificance. We learned that when we feel like a nobody going nowhere, it is simply not true. We learned that he was part of the creative process, "weaving us together in our mother's womb" for his purposes and for our good. Did you know that Jesus was directly involved in the creative process? The New Testament clearly says, "All things were created by him and for him. He is before all things, and in him all things hold together (Col. 1:16b–17a). That includes you.

He knows you and understands you like no one else in the world. He has a plan for your life, and he's watching over you day by day. You are important to him. You are special and significant. The Scriptures tell us that when Jesus died upon the cross, he paid for your sin so that he might redeem you, adopt you, and make you part of his family. If you have received him as Lord and Savior, he has sealed you with his Spirit and has deposited within you certain spiritual gifts so that you might serve him according to your unique design. Jesus reminds you that, far from being insignificant, you are one of a kind. He will help you discover the beauty that he's created within you and the purposes he has created for you (see Eph. 1:14; 2:8–10).

Psalm 77—Jesus Is Your Deliverer

In Psalm 77 we learned that one of the ways to overcome depression involves looking in the rearview mirror of our lives in order to be reminded of God's past deliverance. The psalmist described how God's mighty hand delivered the people out of trouble. God worked supernaturally then and he can do it now. Jesus' life was characterized by miracles that confirmed his identity as the Son of God. Far beyond delivering people from depres-

245

sion, he actually healed the sick, fed the hungry, and raised people from the dead.

Jesus delivered people from sin. In your time of deepest trouble and depression, Jesus wants you to know that he will be with you. He has power to deliver you. He understands those dark nights of the soul that are more oppressive than any sickness or problem we may encounter. Scripture tells us that he experienced every temptation, including depression, yet was without sin (see Heb. 2:14–18; 4:14–16; 5:7–10). These passages reveal that Jesus cried out to God with many tears and learned obedience in the school of suffering. Jesus spent time in the trenches, the muck, and the mire, so that we would know that God is able "to sympathize with our weaknesses" (Heb. 4:15).

When we're depressed, we long to talk to someone who has the power to help us see life as it truly is, rather than how we perceive it to be. In times of depression and trouble, Jesus invites you to take his hand, follow him, and let him deliver you from the darkest pit. You see, the great Deliverer of the Old Testament is the compassionate and understanding Deliverer of the New Testament—Jesus. When Jesus said, "I am with you always," part of what that meant was his promise to deliver us.

Psalm 46—Jesus Is Your Refuge

In Psalm 46 we learned that God is an ever-present help in times of need. He will be our fortress and refuge. God will also be a river that represents his presence and power even during times when we are attacked. Today Jesus makes the same offer to every follower in the body of Christ. As you follow him, he says to you, "I will never ever leave you or forsake you" (see Heb. 13:5). He told his disciples after commanding them to make disciples of all the nations, "I am with you always, to the very end of the age" (Matt. 28:20b). When you are gripped by fear, he invites you to draw near to him, and he promises to draw near to you (see James 4:8).

When the troubles of the world or threats of terrorism or economic doom cause you anxiety, Jesus says, "I am with you always." When tensions at home and struggles with children threaten to overwhelm you, Jesus says, "I am with you always." When baggage from your past produces such oppressive fear that you can't take steps that you know are right and good, Jesus whispers in your ear, "Step out with me. I am with you always."

Psalm 51—Jesus Is Your Savior

In Psalm 51 we learned that God has a plan for those who have blown it big time. When we've sinned and done what we know we shouldn't have, he is there. When we've sinned by not doing what we should have, God is there. We learned that though God is a holy and just judge, he is also eager to forgive. The very moment we come to him honestly and repentantly and ask for his forgiveness, the God of the universe springs into action on our behalf and meets us at our point of greatest need. He forgives, cleanses, and restores.

Scripture says that Jesus came to seek and to save that which was lost (see Luke 19:10). He said that he did not come for those who are healthy, but for those who are sick and in trouble (see Matt. 9:10–13). Jesus died upon the cross to pay for your sin and for mine. When we, his followers, find ourselves overwhelmed with guilt and shame, we feel distant from God. At these times, Jesus says to us, "Confess your sin to me." His promise is that he will forgive us and cleanse us from all unrighteousness (see 1 John 1:9). The more we are aware of the distance between ourselves and God, which is created by our sin, the farther Jesus reaches across the gulf with compassion and forgiveness to say, "I will be with you always."

Psalm 90—Jesus Is Your Friend

In Psalm 90 we learned that God's antidote for confusion is to think clearly, biblically, and accurately about the big issues of life. Moses discovered these truths in his friendship with God.

247

Throughout Scripture this process is called acquiring wisdom. It's learning to live according to God's design—fully conscious of God's greatness, life's brevity, sin's seriousness, and the mercy that is available for each one of us. The results of wise living include a well-invested life, the experience of joy, and making an impact for good in the world. Isn't it refreshing to discover that God's ways are not a list of mechanical practices we must glean from an ancient book?

God's wisdom comes through a personal relationship with him and flows into every other relationship in our lives. The same God who called Moses friend is willing to call us friends. Jesus said to his followers on the last night before his death, "I no longer call you servants, because a servant does not know his master's business. Instead, I have called you friends, for everything that I learned from my Father I have made known to you" (John 15:15). Jesus wants to make known to you how to live, what to do, and how to do it. He longs to be your friend.

Scripture tells us that we actually have the mind (or attitude) of Christ (see 1 Cor. 2:16, Phil. 2:5), and that the Spirit of God will lead us into all truth as Jesus takes up residence within our lives (see John 16:8–11). There are many things in life that we don't understand, and we need wisdom to make good decisions. Jesus invites you to find clarity in the midst of confusion. He wants to be your friend. He wants to lead you through his Word. He wants to talk to you when you pray and comfort you when you are confused. During times of confusion we need to hear Jesus say, "Come to me, all you who are weary and burdened, and I will give you rest. Take my yoke upon you and learn from me, for I am gentle and humble in heart, and you will find rest for your souls. For my yoke is easy and my burden is light" (Matt. 11:28–30).

EXPERIENCING GOD ALWAYS

So let me ask, would you like to experience God all the time, every day? Would you like to encounter God, not only in times of crisis but also in times of good and plenty? Would you like to know God in a personal way and have him speak to you, lead you, and encourage you? Would you like to know that you are not alone no matter what happens to those you love or what occurs in the rest of the world? Would you like to know for sure that there is a place reserved for you in heaven and that you can have an eternal hope that will never fade away? Would you like to sense God's presence and power as you drive to work, as you talk to people, as you relate to your family, or as you live out your singleness before a watching world?

All these questions are not an exercise in spiritual futility. They are all possible. In fact, they are more than possible! For those who know Christ personally, he made an awesome promise that is available to every believer. His promise is, "I will be with you always." Jesus' real presence in your life is the "how" to every one of those questions above.

If you are uncertain about how this works, let me give you a brief overview. I also encourage you to talk to the most committed Christians you know and ask questions about how to experience God moment by moment, every day. But to get you started,

I will give you a few basics (we always need to start with basics) on how to experience God each and every day:

- ✓ *Spend time daily reading his Word.* Jesus said, "Man does not live by bread alone, but on every word that comes from the mouth of God" (Matt. 4:4). It may be a new experience for you, but as you quietly sit and read small portions of Scripture and think about them at length, God will begin to reveal himself to you. As you study the life of Christ and read through the New Testament, you will discover how to build a personal and intimate relationship with Jesus.

- ✓ *Spend time each day telling God what's on your heart and asking for his help.* The Bible calls this prayer. Jesus gives us a model for praying in Luke 11:2–4, traditionally called the Lord's Prayer. Studying this prayer will teach you how to address God and will highlight the most important aspects of your conversation with him. But most of all, when you pray, be honest and genuine. Tell God what matters to you. Thank him for what he's doing in your life, and ask for his help in every situation that you are facing. You will be amazed at how God intervenes in your life and circumstances.

- ✓ *Find a good, Bible-teaching church.* Get involved in a community of believers. You see, once we come to know Christ personally, his Spirit dwells in us. That means that one of the most fundamental ways Jesus will reveal himself to you is through other people. The body that Jesus lived in when he walked upon the earth had hands, feet, arms, and eyes through which he touched, healed, and cared for people. The body that he occupies in our day is the body of Christ, what we call the church. Today Jesus touches our lives through the hands, feet, and gifts of brothers and sisters in his body. Simply going to church, however, is not enough. It's in the deep, intimate relationships of biblical community where you will experience the power and the presence of Christ. Others will also experience the presence and power of Christ through you.

- ✓ *Look for opportunities to express God's love to others.* As you serve others, whether it's meeting a physical need, lending a listening ear, or reaching out to someone who is troubled, you will experience God's presence with you. Jesus wants to help you and lead you, but he also wants to accomplish his purposes through you. How it all works exactly, I really don't know. But this I do know—as we give love and concern to others, God in turn gives love and concern back to us.

The above are very basic steps in experiencing the personal promise of Jesus to "be with you always." My prayer is you will experience freshness in your relationship with Christ and you will grasp more fully the depth of his love for you.

I have a few final words for you who picked up this book and are not yet certain whether or not you have a relationship with Christ. Let's go back for a moment to the beginning of this chapter. I was in the bathtub asking God to heal my leg. As I said, that's the earliest memory I have of crying out to God. I knew what I wanted God to do, but God knew what I really needed. He didn't give me the answer I wanted; he gave me something better—the first pangs of a hunger for him. You see, this wasn't just the first time I called out to God; it was the first time I realized that life was about more than I could accomplish on my own. Until that moment, my life had revolved around sports. If God had instantly healed my leg, I would have been back on the court within minutes. I probably wouldn't have gone to church to thank God; I would have gone to the gym to continue practicing my own religion.

God didn't have anything against baseball and basketball. He simply knew that sports couldn't remain the center of my life; he had other plans for me. So my leg became a constant reminder that things like baseball and basketball can be fun, but they are not eternal. They are not valuable in the same way that life is valuable.

But here's the rest of the story and an example of God's humor. Eventually, the problem with my leg significantly cleared up, and I was able to compete again in sports. Three years later, I was able to attend a summer training camp with the Fellowship of Christian Athletes. The staff for this camp was made up of well-known and very successful professional athletes who were deeply com-

251

mitted to Jesus Christ. They introduced me to a grown-up Jesus who understood me in all the ways we have been discussing in these pages. These godly men showed me for the first time that even great athletes don't have to worship sports. They taught me through their example and their words what it really meant to be a Christian. They invited me to become their brother in Christ. I said yes. It was the best decision I ever made. After graduating from college, I was privileged to represent Christ on a traveling team that visited many countries, playing basketball games in order to get the opportunity to share Jesus Christ.

I know God heard my prayer from the bathtub and answered it. I'm still amazed at the answer. My relationship with him today is a wonderful and complicated result of that day. He used that moment of extreme need to get me moving in the right direction, even though I was still far from where he wanted me to be.

I can't help but think that some who are reading this book find themselves in the same place. Your understanding and awareness of God has only involved moments of crisis and need. Now you are wondering if a daily, healthy, joyful life in Christ is a possibility for you. It certainly is!

Have You Met Him?

Here's my last question. I know you have asked God for things. I know you have probably called out to him in moments of crisis and need. Have you ever actually met him? There's a huge difference between asking a stranger for help and asking your best friend. Asking someone you hardly know for a favor isn't at all like asking someone who has been with you in a relationship for a long time. The place to start a personal relationship with Christ is the same place where any relationship starts—an introduction.

Meeting Christ doesn't mean you know everything about him. It means you know enough to decide that you want that relationship more than you want anything else. It means you understand that the gospel applies to you and that you wholeheartedly accept Jesus' invitation to trust him with your life and your destiny.

252

First, you need to know that God, in Christ, has already done something for you that you could never do for yourself. That's the good news. In order to understand why this is good news, you have to hear the bad news.

You see, the Bible clearly teaches that we've all sinned and fallen short of the glory of God (Rom. 3:23). Your sin and my sin separate us from a holy God. Sin is a debt that keeps getting larger, and we have no way to make a payment. The best we can do is not counted as extra credit; it's only what we're supposed to do. We're spiritually bankrupt.

Unless we get outside help, the consequences of our spiritual bankruptcy are predictable—punishment and death and eternal separation from God. The first half of Romans 6:23 describes these results succinctly: "For the wages of sin is death." Fortunately, the good news comes in the second half of that verse. Outside help is available and it's absolutely free. "For the wages of sin is death, **but the gift of God is eternal life in Christ Jesus our Lord.**"

You may wonder how eternal life can be a free gift to sinners. Well, it's free to us, but it cost someone a lot. As we have seen in the Psalms, God is holy and just. Sin must be punished. God's love doesn't cover or overwhelm his holiness. Someone must pay the penalty, or in the language of Romans 6:23, someone must accept the wages of sin that we earned. Someone must take our place. That someone was Jesus.

The Bible teaches that when Jesus died on the cross, he paid for your sin and mine once and for all, "in our place" (Rom. 5:8). He settled our account (see Col. 2:13–15). The death of Christ is God's gift of grace toward you. Nothing you or I could ever do can merit God's favor. Being a good person, trying hard, going to church, or attempting to do good works can never make us acceptable to God. Jesus emphatically stated, "I am the way and the truth and the life. No one comes to the Father except through me" (John 14:6). Jesus was fully God and fully man, so in his death on the cross, he fully represented us and fully paid the debt of sin once and for all.

But simply knowing what Christ has done does not place you in a relationship with him. Admitting your sin is the first step. Understanding the just consequences of your sin is the next step.

Realizing that Christ has paid for your sin once and for all is the third step. But it doesn't stop there. *You must personally receive God's gift by faith.* The Scriptures declare, "Yet to all who received him, to those who believed in his name, he gave the right to become children of God" (John 1:12). You must receive the gift, not simply know about it. If you have never received him, Jesus is saying to you at this moment, **"Here I am! I stand at the door and knock. If anyone hears my voice and opens the door, I will come in and eat with him, and he with me"** (Rev. 3:20).

This is the offer that the eternal God makes to you through Jesus Christ. He wants to be with you always. And he wants you to be with him always. Why? Because he loves you!

So the ball's in your court. What will you do with this marvelous and amazing offer of forgiveness of your sins and a relationship with God through Jesus Christ? Will you pray right now to receive him into your life? Will you admit your sin and turn from it?

You can come to God right now through Jesus Christ. You can, through a brief prayer, express the earnest desire of your heart to become a member of God's family. If you are willing, you might pray in this way:

> *Dear God,*
>
> *I admit today that I'm a sinner. I know that I've done many things wrong and hurt many people. I deserve to be punished for my sin, but I believe that Christ died to pay for my sin, if I would but receive his sacrifice as a gift. Right now I trust that Christ took my place in his death, and that by his resurrection, he guaranteed his offer of eternal life to me. I receive you into my life right now as my Savior. Help me to become the man, the woman, or young person that you want me to be. Help me to walk with you all the days of my life.*
>
> *Thank you, Almighty God, that from this day forward I will never be alone. Thank you for being with me always. Amen.*

NOTES

Chapter 2: In Times of Crisis

1. Phillip Keller, *A Shepherd Looks at Psalm 23* (New York: HarperCollins, 1970), 81.

Chapter 4: When You Are Troubled and Depressed

1. Signg-Yang Tan, "The ABC's of Depression: A Review of the Basics," *Christian Counseling Today*, fall 1995, 10.

2. Stephen Arterburn and Connie Neal, *The Emotional Freedom Workbook* (Nashville: Thomas Nelson, 1997).

3. Dr. Paul Meier, Dallas Theological Seminary (class notes and personal interviews), 1981.

4. Ibid.

5. Paul D. Meier, M.D., Frank B. Wichern, Ph.D., and Frank B. Minirth, M.D., *Introduction to Psychology and Counseling* (Grand Rapids: Baker, 1982).

6. Meier, Dallas Theological Seminary.

7. Ibid.

Chapter 5: When You Are Gripped by Fear

1. Oskar Thulin, ed. and comp., *A Life of Luther: Told in Pictures and Narrative by the Reformer and His Contemporaries,* trans. Martin O. Dietrich (Philadelphia: Fortress, 1966), 58.

Chapter 6: When You've Blown It Big Time

1. Stephen Arterburn and David Stoop, *Seven Keys to Spiritual Renewal* (Wheaton: Tyndale, 1998), 56–58.

Chip Ingram (Th.M., Dallas Theological Seminary) is senior pastor of Santa Cruz Bible Church on California's Monterey Bay. His popular radio program, *Living on the Edge,* can be heard on hundreds of stations nationwide, and on the Internet at www.lote.org. Chip and his wife, Theresa, are the parents of three sons and one daughter.